THE BIG, BOLD, ADVENTUROUS LIFE OF
LAVINIA WARREN

ELIZABETH RAUM

CHICAGO
REVIEW
PRESS

Copyright © 2018 by Elizabeth Raum
All rights reserved
Published by Chicago Review Press Incorporated
814 North Franklin Street
Chicago, Illinois 60610
ISBN 978-0-912777-50-4

Library of Congress Cataloging-in-Publication Data
Names: Raum, Elizabeth, author.
Title: The big, bold, adventurous life of Lavinia Warren / Elizabeth Raum.
Description: Chicago, Illinois : Chicago Review Press, 2018. | Includes
  bibliographical references and index. | Audience: Age 10 and up.
Identifiers: LCCN 2017060546 (print) | LCCN 2018002354 (ebook) | ISBN
  9780912777511 (adobe pdf) | ISBN 9780912777528 (kindle) | ISBN
  9780912777535 (epub) | ISBN 9780912777504 (cloth)
Subjects: LCSH: Magri, M. Lavinia (Mercy Lavinia), 1841–1919—Juvenile
  literature. | Women circus performers—United States—Biography—Juvenile
  literature.
Classification: LCC GV1811.M335 (ebook) | LCC GV1811.M335 R38 2018 (print) |
  DDC 791.3092 [B] —dc23
LC record available at https://lccn.loc.gov/2017060546

Interior design: Sarah Olson

Printed in the United States of America
5 4 3 2 1

CONTENTS

INTRODUCTION

Lavinia Warren never grew taller than a yardstick. In fact, she was shorter than most three-year-olds. Tasks that most of us take for granted proved nearly impossible for her. She couldn't reach the kitchen sink, and sitting on a normal-sized sofa meant climbing up—unless a kind friend gave her a lift. Store-bought clothing never fit. Everything had to be specially made—her dresses, shoes, hats, and gloves. Daily life was filled with obstacles for Lavinia Warren.

In addition to the difficulties posed by her size, Lavinia lived during tumultuous times. The ongoing debate over slavery erupted into violence even before the Civil War began, and Lavinia was caught in the middle of it. She survived, and so did the nation, but the war left its mark on everyone living in America in the mid-1800s.

Despite her tiny size, and in part because of it, Lavinia performed for audiences around the world. She was as famous in her day as movie stars are today. She touched the lives of thousands of people in hundreds of places during her adventurous life. People marveled at her size, her poise, and her dignity. Being small was never an excuse for Lavinia Warren. It was simply a fact of life, a life that began in a small village in eastern Massachusetts.

LIVING LIFE SMALL

There were lots of Bumps in Middleborough, Massachusetts, and every one of them was tall. James Bump was over six feet tall. His wife, Huldah, was tall too. Their first four children grew as tall and slender as corn in August. On October 31, 1841, a fifth baby Bump was born. Her parents named her Mercy Lavinia Warren Bump. At birth, Mercy weighed six pounds. Everyone assumed that she would become a big Bump too.

But around the time of her first birthday, Mercy stopped growing—or at least she slowed way down. It took her five years to grow as much as most children grow in a single year. At age 10, Mercy measured 24 inches tall and weighed 20 pounds. Many two-year-olds were bigger. Her fourth-grade classmates towered above her.

No one knew what caused Mercy to stop growing, not in 1842. Today, doctors know that children like

Mercy lack a certain growth hormone. Mercy's medical condition was called dwarfism. There are more than 200 different kinds of dwarfism. Mercy was a proportionate dwarf. *Proportionate* means that all the parts of her body were small to the same degree. She looked like other children except that she was much, much smaller.

Mercy's parents accepted her just as she was. They sent her to the local school, took her to church on Sundays, and insisted that she help with chores around the house. Although her parents tried to treat her exactly as they had treated their other children, they had to make allowances for her small size.

Her father, James, was a farmer and often carried her on his arm when he went to the barn to care for the cattle. To make life easier for her, he built a lightweight set of steps so she could reach the kitchen countertop and fetch items from the cabinets. She could move the steps from place to place whenever she needed them. Mercy's mother, Huldah, taught her to sew her own clothes, embroider, and knit her own sweaters. Mercy especially enjoyed embroidery and other kinds of needlework.

It wasn't always easy for someone so small to handle household chores, but Mercy was smart. She figured out how to get things done. Sometimes she had to remind her mother that she couldn't accomplish a particular task because of her size. But little setbacks didn't stop Mercy Bump. She wanted to please her parents and live up to their expectations. When she wrote her autobiography, she dedicated it to them:

To the memory of my
Father and Mother,
to whom I owe a happy childhood and whose
integrity and uprightness has given me a
standard which, if often my arrow falls
below, has held me to the motto
"Aim high."

SCHOOL DAYS

Middleborough was a small town; everyone knew everyone else. When Mercy went off to school the first day with her brothers and sisters, her size was no surprise to her classmates. She was as bright and capable as the other students; she was simply much smaller.

To reach her desk, Mercy sat on a high stool. Most of the time, she worked hard at her studies. Sometimes, however, she quietly climbed down to play tricks on the others. She would run beneath the desks and give her classmates tiny pinches. They gasped or squealed in surprise until they realized that it was Mercy, and then they sputtered and giggled.

Mr. Dunbar, the teacher, was not amused. By the time the tall, gangly teacher crouched down to identify the culprit, Mercy had already darted back to her seat. Mr. Dunbar would find her sitting quietly at her desk, hard at work, and with an angelic look on her face. That didn't fool Mr. Dunbar. He knew exactly who had caused the trouble. "What shall I do with you? Shall I shut you in my overshoe?" he asked. "What does your mother do with you? Does she set you on top of the sugar bowl and make you wipe the dishes?" One day, after some such mischief, Mr. Dunbar plunked Mercy down on top of the biggest dictionary he could find. He glanced at the giant book from time to time to make sure that his smallest pupil stayed put.

Despite her good sense of humor and her generally cheerful nature, Mercy didn't like being different. For a while at least, she tried to behave. She found it embarrassing when the teacher, or anyone, commented about her size. Even so, temptation soon called out to her. Mercy was the perfect messenger, so her classmates asked her to carry notes for them. She would sneak beneath the desks and place the forbidden notes directly into the children's hands. Mr. Dunbar didn't see a thing, at least not most of the time.

MINNIE

When Mercy was seven years old, her sister was born. The baby's name was Huldah Pierce Warren Bump, but the family called her Minnie. Would this baby grow to be as tall as her older brothers and sisters, or would she be as tiny as Mercy? The answer soon became apparent. Like Mercy, Minnie stopped growing when she was about a year old. The two smallest Bumps became best friends. Here, at last, was someone who looked up to Mercy. The rest of the world, even children who were much younger, looked down at her.

Mercy included Minnie in her pranks. In her autobiography, Mercy writes about the day she "borrowed" the peddler's wagon and took Minnie for a wild ride. In those days, peddlers traveled door-to-door selling pots, wooden items, and brooms from the back of a wagon. One day a peddler stopped at the Bump home. Mercy and Minnie were playing outside while the peddler sat in the kitchen visiting with their parents. Mercy suggested a ride in the peddler's wagon. Little Minnie agreed.

It was no easy task for the tiny girls to climb into the wagon. Mercy had to push, tug, and pull Minnie up the steep steps onto the wagon's seat. When both girls were perched on the big seat, Mercy put her arm around Minnie and grabbed the horse's reins. The thick reins were far too large for Mercy's tiny hands, but she was determined to take her little sister for a ride. When Mercy said, "Get up! Go 'long!" the horse trotted off, pulling the wagon down the hill toward town.

Crunch. Crackle. Crunch. The sounds of the wagon wheels alerted the adults that something was amiss. By the time they ran outside, the wagon was bumping down the gravel road. Onlookers saw what they thought were two dolls bouncing precariously on the wagon's wooden seat.

Mercy gripped her sister and the seat, still urging the horse forward. "It required my utmost strength to retain my hold upon Minnie and cling to the seat," she later wrote, "and it was a wonder we were not thrown upon the road."

One of their older brothers ran to the stable for a horse. He leaped onto the horse bareback and raced to rescue the girls. He caught up with the wagon a mile from home, grabbed the reins, and pulled the runaway horse to a halt. Luckily it was a gentle creature. As Mercy later wrote,

We were in high glee, laughing and enjoying the fun, but my brother took us back and I received a long lecture upon the danger I had incurred, and a promise [never to do it again].

The peddler, after examining his wares and finding no damage, treated the matter as a good joke, saying "I have owned that horse for 12 years and the greatest speed I could get out of him was three miles an hour, but I now believe that the animal is a racer."

LITTLE MISS BUMP, TEACHER

Mercy did so well in school that she graduated early. When she was 16, members of the local school board came to call. They were seeking a teacher for the primary students, children aged four through nine. In the 1850s, teachers were not required to go to college or to hold teaching degrees. The school board knew Mercy and trusted her. They knew she was clever enough to teach the younger students. They offered her the job, and she accepted.

Even the youngest students were taller than Miss Bump. Mercy made it clear that although she was small, she was in charge. She stood on a table to teach. She later wrote, "The youngest even was far above me in stature,

This undated photo shows Mercy Bump as a young girl.

yet all seemed anxious to be obedient and to please me."
Her students mastered their lessons, followed the rules,
and never took advantage of their tiny teacher. In fact,
they did what they could to make life easier for her. On
muddy days, the big boys clasped their hands together to
make a seat for Miss Bump. They carried her over deep
puddles. On snowy days, they pulled her to school on a
sled.

Teaching suited Mercy. She enjoyed it. She was naturally reserved, meticulous in her appearance, and dainty.
Children and parents respected her. At the end of the
school year, the district school committee thanked her
for an excellent job. Mercy thought that she had found
the perfect career. But a surprise visit from a distant
cousin changed the course of Mercy's life.

AN UNEXPECTED OFFER

George Wood visited Middleborough during the summer vacation. He'd heard about his little cousin and
wanted to meet her. It was more than just a friendly
visit; Wood planned to offer Mercy a very different
opportunity.

Wood, who was called Colonel Wood by his employees, worked for the Spaulding and Rogers's North
American Circus, a company that sailed showboats up
and down the Ohio and Mississippi Rivers. Showboats
provided entertainment for people living in river towns

This studio portrait shows Lavinia as a young woman.

and villages. Showboats often included what were called museums. These museums featured displays of animals or birds, often stuffed. But the main displays were people labeled "living curiosities" or, unkindly, "freaks" or "human oddities."

People are often curious about those who are different. In the mid-1800s, people who were unusually tall or short, fat or thin, sometimes found work as living curiosities. So did people born with missing limbs or extra limbs. People with developmental disabilities, conjoined twins, and those with extra hair (such as bearded women) were hired as curiosities. In addition to those on showboats, some of these so-called museums were located on land in major cities. Shows that featured living curiosities were called "freak shows." At the time, knowledge of science and medicine was increasing rapidly. Doctors and scientists often visited such shows to learn more about unusual conditions. Their comments and interest spurred others to go too. Showmen took advantage of people's curiosity.

George Wood knew that people would find Mercy fascinating because of her size. He offered her a job as a curiosity on Spaulding and Rogers's Floating Palace of Curiosities. She would meet and greet the people in river towns who paid to come aboard the showboat. George assured her family that Mercy would become famous, not just in America but also throughout the world. At the time, no one guessed that his prediction would come true.

A Curious Opportunity

As a child, Mercy had been embarrassed about her size, but her cousin's proposal intrigued her. It ignited her sense of adventure. Sailing unfamiliar rivers on a steamboat and meeting interesting people stirred her imagination. So did the idea of exploring the West.

Most of those who were called living curiosities had no other choice than to accept a job as a "freak." Colonel Wood's showboat—and others like it—gave people who were born different an opportunity to make a living. Managers and showmen paid good wages and provided room and board. The curiosities developed their own communities within the world of show business. Mercy, however, had a choice. She had proved her worth as a teacher; she could continue making a good living in a respected profession, or she could accept Colonel Wood's curious offer.

Wood promised Mercy's family that he would protect her—with his life, if necessary. He would provide whatever she needed or wanted while she was in his care. He argued with passion, and he seemed sincere.

With adventure in mind, Mercy chose to leave teaching behind and become a performer—if her parents would give their blessing. They looked to their eldest son for advice. He argued against the plan. He felt that Mercy's life would be in danger. Showboats sometimes burned and sank. The towns along the river were rough, and rowdy crowds flocked onto the showboats. Mercy was too small to protect herself, her brother said, and she would be alone in a big and scary world. Mercy's parents listened closely to their son's arguments. He was right, they thought. Mercy could be in danger.

Mercy waited patiently. Her parents knew that she was confident. They knew that she was curious and craved adventure. They had always treated her as they treated their other children, and she had proved herself to be responsible and self-reliant. In addition, George Wood had promised to protect her. Mercy wanted to go. How could they say no? Finally, if somewhat reluctantly, they agreed to let her accept her cousin's offer.

A NEW NAME FOR A NEW LIFE

In April 1858, Mercy bid farewell to friends and family. She exchanged the safety they offered for a life of adventure. Everything was about to change, even her name. She wanted an elegant name, something with a more theatrical ring than *Mercy Bump*.

Mercy was particularly proud of the name Warren. Two of her ancestors had played major roles in American history. The first was Richard Warren. He had come to America on the *Mayflower* in 1620, signed the Mayflower Compact, and was one of the original settlers of Plymouth Colony.

The second was Dr. Joseph Warren, an American patriot. Dr. Warren had been a well-respected physician practicing in Boston just before the outbreak of the Revolutionary War. His patients included John Adams, Paul Revere, and William Dawes, all of whom became leaders during the Revolution. Dr. Warren felt that a doctor's duties extended beyond medicine. He became a trusted spokesperson in the colonies' fight for independence from the British. He worked with Paul Revere to organize America's first spy network—the very group that warned the Massachusetts towns of Lexington and Concord that the British were coming in April 1775. The next day, the first shots of the Revolutionary War were fired. Dr. Warren was a member of the Continental Congress, and on June 14, 1775, he was appointed a major general. He died during the Battle of Bunker Hill while providing cover for retreating American soldiers.

Mercy considered both of these ancestors genuine American heroes. She decided to use the name Warren as a surname and Lavinia as her first name. After all, her parents had chosen these names when she was born, and Mercy loved and respected her family. Using names they had chosen honored them as well as her ancestors. She became Lavinia Warren. Eventually, even her family called her Lavinia or Vinnie.

THE FLOATING PALACE

George Wood was as good as his word. He escorted Lavinia safely to Cincinnati, Ohio, where the Floating Palace of Curiosities was anchored. The Floating Palace was the most spectacular showboat of them all. It

This 1850s drawing shows the Floating Palace as it appeared when Lavinia joined the company.

was a combination floating theater, minstrel hall, and museum. The showboat was 200 feet long. (That's more than twice as long as a professional basketball court.) Two hundred gas lamps lit the interior. The showboat's central theater had 1,000 seats on the main deck, another 1,500 seats on a second level called the family circle, and another 900 seats set aside for African American customers. People came aboard to watch singers, dancers, and other entertainers put on variety shows and plays. There was also an animal show featuring performing horses. The museum claimed to house 100,000 items from the past. Lavinia and the other living curiosities appeared in the museum area as well. The showboat included a stable for the animals and bedrooms, called staterooms, for the performers and staff.

Lavinia was to share one of the showboat's staterooms with Miss Sylvia Hardy. Lavinia's first look at Sylvia sent fearful tremors through her body. Miss Hardy was a giant! She was eight feet tall, almost five feet taller than Lavinia. The stateroom was not only Lavinia's bedroom; it was where she spent her free time. Years later, Lavinia wrote in her autobiography, "My heart failed me at the thought that I was to be almost continually in her company."

Soon, however, the giant and the dwarf became great friends. Lavinia later wrote, "I was with her [Sylvia] but a short time when I learned to love her and to realize that her great body was quite a necessity if it was to contain her large heart." When Lavinia suffered one of her frequent headaches, Sylvia would lift Lavinia onto her huge lap and soothe her to sleep as if she were a small child.

The friendship between Lavinia and Sylvia was not unusual. Despite their great size difference, they had much in common. They were both objects of curiosity, and they both faced difficulties related to their size. The world was too big for Lavinia's comfort and too small for Sylvia's.

The illustration on the cover of an 1856 biography of Sylvia Hardy shows her standing next to an average-sized woman.

BECOMING AN ENTERTAINER

Lavinia became an instant success. Newspaper reports described her as "one of the most extraordinary little ladies at any time seen in this age of extraordinary beings" and encouraged everyone to go see her. She visited with the people who came aboard. She was an excellent conversationalist and a talented singer.

Lavinia had been singing since childhood. When she was in school, she sang at school events. She stood on a desk to perform. "I thought I could sing," she said years later, "I was young then—and sang at these entertainments." She continued singing throughout her stage career.

Handbills advertising the show were sent to towns along the river before the showboat arrived. By the time the Floating Palace reached the dock, crowds were waiting to purchase tickets. Once the customers were on board, the boat sailed up and down the river. Ticket holders visited the museum, attended the show, and strolled along the deck. When the boat returned to town, the passengers disembarked.

DODGING ROCKS AND BULLETS

Frequently, when the showboat returned to the dock, some of the entertainers got off to stretch their legs or to buy a drink in the local tavern. Not Lavinia. She rarely left the showboat. She felt safest there—and with good reason. Trouble often followed when a showboat came to town. As Lavinia wrote years later, "In those years there was usually a rough element in almost every town who considered that there had been no fun 'without a fight with the showmen' as a finale."

In her memoir, Lavinia describes one such time. Several ruffians attacked a group of male performers as they walked through town. The performers managed to escape and race back to the boat. Their attackers followed them, shouting insults. At the river, the entertainers jumped onto the deck of the showboat. The moment that the last performer hit the deck, the crew pulled up the gangway. Eventually, the crowd dispersed, promising to return in the morning.

It was only a short distance to the next scheduled stop. The boat's captain hadn't planned to leave until 10:00 the next morning, but he quickly changed his plans. He ordered the boat to steam away at sunrise. Even so, Lavinia wrote, "Early as it was, we were awakened by a howling, yelling mob on the levee, armed with guns and pistols." They demanded that the performers come back and finish the fight. When no one responded, the crowd threw stones and fired their guns at the showboat.

Lavinia shook with fear. "Our terror soon increased," she wrote, "for the angry mob hurriedly secured planks and there was every indication that they would be successful in their design to come on board the boat. To our great joy, at that moment the engines began to move and slowly but surely the boat drew away."

The performers had the last laugh. When the boat pulled away, the hastily placed planks fell into the water. So did the men standing on them. Someone on shore fired one final round. The bullet made a neat hole in the hat of the ship's pilot, but it missed its mark. It didn't even ruffle the man's hair. The showboat sailed off to its next port, hoping for a happier reception there.

At first this kind of trouble upset Lavinia. This was not the excitement she sought. As time went on, however, she was able to relax and enjoy the adventure. After all, she was getting good reviews. A reporter from a St. Louis newspaper, the *Daily Missouri Democrat*, wrote in a July 17, 1858, article:

> Among the six living wonders now exhibiting, none seem to win more general attention and admiration than the fairy Queen of Lilliput, Miss Warren. She is, indeed, a most extraordinary little creature. She is not only exceedingly small—measuring only some 28 inches—but perfectly formed, and as beautiful and lovely as a sylph [a slender, graceful woman or girl]. Ladies, gentlemen, boys and girls throng around her in rapt admiration.—The bearded Lady and the infant Esau are passing strange, and the American Giantess looms up like a huge tower, but the little Queen is, after all, the attraction of them all, and the cynosure [center of attention] of all eyes.—The rain of Monday kept away

many who desired to see her, but yesterday they poured in, in a steady stream from 9 o'clock in the morning until 9 o'clock in the evening. All parents should allow their children to go and see this extraordinary freak of nature, for a lifetime might not give them another opportunity.

LILLIPUT

When the reporter called Lavinia the "Queen of Lilliput," he was referring to Jonathan Swift's 1726 novel *Gulliver's Travels*. Swift created an island called Lilliput. The inhabitants were about six inches tall.

IMPORTANT VISITORS

Handbills and newspaper articles attracted admiring crowds wherever the Floating Palace docked. It seemed as if everyone wanted to meet the "little queen." On her very first trip up the Mississippi, the Floating Palace stopped at Galena, Illinois. One of those who came aboard was Ulysses S. Grant. Grant had retired from the US Army a few years earlier and moved his family to Galena. When Lavinia met him, he worked in his father's leather store. Later, he rejoined the army and became a leading general during the Civil War. Later still, from 1869 to 1877, he was president of the United States.

Lavinia impressed Grant so much that he purchased her photograph and asked for her autograph. The next day he returned with his entire family. They visited for a while and then, as they left, they wished her well on her journey.

Ulysses S. Grant (seated in the center) and his family on their porch in Galena, Illinois.

Thousands visited the Floating Palace, but Lavinia took special note of Grant. Years later she recalled his visit with pride. She would meet him again during the Civil War, and many years later at the White House when he was serving as president.

A BRUSH WITH DEATH

From time to time, Lavinia suffered from severe headaches. Other than that, she was generally healthy. However, early in 1859 she developed a fever. Over the course of several days, the fever grew worse and Lavinia grew weaker. Doctors at various river towns examined her. They diagnosed typhoid fever, a life-threatening illness caused by exposure to someone with the disease or by eating or drinking contaminated food or water. There was no cure at the time.

Lavinia's fever raged for three months. Lizzie Edmunds, the wife of one of the minstrels, took on the role of nursing Lavinia through the illness. Lizzie placed

ANTIBIOTICS

Today, doctors treat typhoid fever with antibiotics. These drugs were not available until 1929 when Alexander Fleming discovered penicillin.

Lavinia on a pillow and held her on her lap through long, feverish nights on the river. She used cool, wet cloths to bring Lavinia's fever down and forced her to sip water and nibble bits of food. Slowly, Lavinia recovered, but it took many weeks for her to regain her former strength.

A VISIT HOME

At some point after her recovery, Lavinia apparently made a brief visit home. A stop in Boston on the way caught the attention of a Boston newspaper. On December 3, 1858, the *Boston Traveler* reported:

> GREAT (?) CURIOSITY.—A rival of Tom Thumb is at present in this city, in the form of a young lady,—Miss Lavinia W. Bump, of Middleboro, who is 18 years old and is only 34 inches in height. She is stopping at the Bromfield House, on her way home from Alabama, after making the tour of 22 States, and in all of which she has been exhibiting.

Even though the reporter added a few inches to Lavinia's height, the story was picked up by her hometown newspaper, the *Middleborough Gazette*, and published there on December 4, 1858. Lavinia fails to mention this visit in her memoirs, but she reports that by the time she was back on the showboat, a war between the states seemed unavoidable.

Ⓓrifting Toward War

As the Floating Palace drifted up and down the rivers, the nation drifted toward war. The debate over slavery was not new to Lavinia or to most Americans of that era. The first African slaves had reached Jamestown, Virginia, in 1619. Since those early days, many states had become dependent on slave labor. By 1776, about 450,000 enslaved people lived in the American colonies. In his first draft of the Declaration of Independence, Thomas Jefferson had wanted to expressly forbid slavery in America. He was not the only one of the nation's founders opposed to slavery even though many of them owned slaves. After a heated discussion, the issue of slavery was left out of the Declaration of Independence. That didn't mean that the problem was resolved. The question was debated right up until the Civil War broke out.

By the late 1700s, slavery had ended in many Northern states; it didn't make economic sense there. Northern farms were small and the farmers did not need slave labor; they did the work themselves. Northern cities and towns were growing, and new industries were forming that took advantage of a steady stream of immigrants from overseas.

Many people believed that slavery would soon die out in the South too. However, in 1793, Eli Whitney invented the cotton gin. Balls of cotton were put into the top of the machine and wire teeth removed the seeds, which made it easier and cheaper to turn cotton into textiles or fabric. Cotton became king, and Southern farmers, unlike those in the North, depended on slave labor to produce huge quantities. By 1860 four million enslaved people worked on Southern cotton plantations. Without them, the South feared economic ruin.

Whenever the United States added new territories or states, the issue of slavery flared again. In 1803 the Louisiana Purchase doubled the size of the United States. Eventually, all or parts of 13 states would be formed out of this vast territory. Should slavery be allowed in the new states?

People on both sides of the issue argued forcefully. In 1820, Congress passed the Missouri Compromise by a vote of 90 to 87. The compromise allowed slavery in the new state of Missouri. In another vote, Congress agreed to forbid slavery in states or territories north of Missouri.

Abolitionists, people who wanted to end slavery, gained strength and political power in the 1850s. Even so, the Fugitive Slave Act of 1850 required everyone in the United States, even in free Northern states, to help capture runaway slaves. Southern plantation owners were pleased; abolitionists were outraged.

In 1854, Stephen A. Douglas, who was Illinois's Democratic senator, introduced the Kansas-Nebraska Act to Congress. The act overturned the Missouri Compromise. Under the act, the residents of each territory would vote on whether to allow slavery. Southern congressmen felt that decisions about slavery should be left to the individual states. Abolitionists disagreed.

Slavery wasn't Stephen Douglas's main concern. He believed that it would eventually end on its own. Rather, he promoted the Kansas-Nebraska Act as a way to gain the support of Southern congressmen on another issue: the transcontinental railroad. Douglas wanted the railroad to take a northern route across the country. Southern congressmen preferred a more southerly route. In exchange for promoting the Kansas-Nebraska Act, Douglas got his railroad, but he did not manage to end the debate over slavery. In fact, the issue grew hotter and hotter until actual battles broke out.

In 1858, Abraham Lincoln and Stephen Douglas engaged in a series of seven debates that became known as the Lincoln-Douglas debates. At the time, they were running against one another for the open Senate seat from Illinois. While they both despised slavery, Douglas wanted to let each state decide for itself whether to allow it. Eventually, he believed, slavery would end. Lincoln feared the spread of slavery to the western states and wanted it ended immediately. Despite these differences, they agreed that the most important goal was to preserve the nation.

When Kansas wanted to join the Union, the issue flared. Should slavery be allowed or not? Northern abolitionists and their supporters went to Kansas, armed and ready to fight. Many who favored slavery poured into Kansas from neighboring Missouri. In all, 55 people died in a battle that became known as Bleeding Kansas. In 1859, Kansas was admitted to the Union as a free state, but the battles were far from over.

THE LITTLE GIANT

Like everyone else in the United States, Lavinia was following the news of the 1860 presidential election with interest. Both candidates were from Illinois. Since the Mississippi River forms the western border of Illinois, the Floating Palace stopped at many towns in that state. During her lifetime, Lavinia had the unique opportunity of meeting both candidates. She met Douglas during the campaign and Lincoln later, after he became president.

When the Floating Palace stopped in Montgomery, Alabama, Stephen Douglas came on board. He had spent many years in Congress before running for president. He was a powerful speaker and a respected politician. Both friends and enemies called him the "Little

Stephen A. Douglas was born in Vermont. At age 20, he moved to Illinois, entered politics, and became that state's US Senator. Eventually, he ran for president as the Democratic candidate against the Republican, Abraham Lincoln.

Giant." Despite his short stature—he was only five feet, four inches tall—he was one of the most powerful men in Congress.

Douglas was enchanted with Lavinia and stooped to kiss her as if she were a child. "I instinctively drew back, feeling my face suffused with blushes," Lavinia wrote in her memoir. "It seemed impossible to make people at first understand that I was not a child." Why, she asked, was that so difficult?

Douglas immediately understood his error. He backed off and began laughing. "I am often called the 'Little Giant,'" he said, "but if I am a giant, I am not necessarily an ogre and will not eat you, although you almost tempt me to do so."

Lavinia laughed. Whatever offense she felt melted away, and she chatted with Douglas for some time. When he left, he wished her continued good health and much happiness.

It was Lavinia's one and only visit with the "Little Giant." Stephen Douglas lost the presidential election. Abraham Lincoln became the 16th president of the United States. The loss broke Douglas's spirit. He died in June 1861, just a few months after Lincoln took office.

TOURING THE SOUTH

During those uneasy days just before the Civil War broke out, the Floating Palace and its troupe of show people continued to cruise along the lower Mississippi River. At one stop Lavinia met Jefferson Davis and his family. Davis was an impressive character. Lavinia described him as "a most chivalrous and kindly gentleman, and I have always looked back to that meeting with pleasure." Davis later became the president of the Confederate States of America. She also met General Robert E. Lee, who led the Confederate army during the Civil War.

At one stop, Mary Lincoln came on board the Floating Palace. She was Abraham Lincoln's wife. Mrs. Lincoln brought her mother with her to the showboat. People present at their meeting commented that Lavinia and Mrs. Lincoln looked alike. Both women were amused. It was a comparison that they would hear again the next time they met. By then, Mrs. Lincoln would be First Lady of the United States.

RUMORS OF WAR

———◇———

Talk of war was impossible to avoid. Everywhere the showboat docked, people were engaged in excited debates over the issues of slavery, states rights, and the impending conflict between North and South.

Lavinia sensed both fear and excitement in this talk. Many Southerners wanted to secede, or leave the United States to form their own government. There were others who wanted to work out the differences and remain a single nation. Many in the North wanted to end slavery, but they didn't want to split the country apart. Rumors of war threw the showboat business into a slump. People had less interest in entertainment. Their time and energy were occupied by far more serious matters.

At the time, the Floating Palace was in southern Mississippi. Most of the entertainers on the showboat were Northerners. Colonel Wood decided that he must get his troupe to safety in the North. What if they were stranded in Mississippi when war broke out? How long would they be trapped in what they considered enemy territory?

Although Lavinia did not discuss her political views in her autobiography, she did not want to remain in the South, far from home, if war broke out. The North was home, and it is likely that Lavinia embraced the Union cause. Eventually her brother served in the Union army.

Colonel Wood acted quickly, in part because many boats—even showboats—were being confiscated or taken for military use. The colonel sold the Floating Palace and used the money to get his performers home. He purchased tickets for his entire troupe on a train headed for Vicksburg, Mississippi.

The train north to Vicksburg took several days. Travel was difficult, and the group often had to switch trains. Some cars were full of guns, ammunition, and other military equipment. It was obvious that the Southern states were gearing up for war.

Finally, Wood and his crew reached Vicksburg safely. From there, they could catch a steamship to Louisville, Kentucky. They checked into a hotel to get some rest before boarding the steamship. Colonel Wood rushed to the ticket office to arrange passage north. Bad news greeted him: the boat going north on the Mississippi River was already full; there were no rooms left. He

WHAT HAPPENED TO THE FLOATING PALACE?

Eventually, the Floating Palace was confiscated. It became a Confederate hospital ship during the Civil War.

refused to give up. After all, he had promised Lavinia's parents that he would protect her, and he intended to do just that.

He forced his way into the ship captain's office. The captain gave the same answer that the ticket agent had given: the ship was full. But Colonel Wood persisted. He begged the captain to come to the hotel and meet the "Little Queen." The boat's captain had undoubtedly seen handbills and heard enthusiastic reports about the "Queen of Lilliput." Wood felt confident that meeting Lavinia would change the captain's mind. The captain, intrigued, agreed to the meeting.

Lavinia wrote, "Whether my size did more for me than my tongue, I never knew," but the captain gave his own cabin to Lavinia and the other women. The men slept on deck. It had been a close call. Lavinia didn't want to imagine what might have happened if she had been stranded far from home in the midst of war.

The troupe reached Louisville without further problems. From there Lavinia and Colonel Wood boarded a train for Massachusetts. He insisted on seeing Lavinia to the front door of her family's home.

By the time Lavinia was safely back in Massachusetts, Abraham Lincoln was president; South Carolina seceded, or left, the Union; and six more states followed: Mississippi, Florida, Alabama, Georgia, Louisiana, and Texas. They formed the Confederate States of America led by President Jefferson Davis. The nation was divided, and President Lincoln seemed determined to go to war.

WITH FAMILY

Lavinia spent the next several months at home with family and friends. She didn't give up show business entirely. She appeared at county and state fairs. But for a while, at least, she relished the safety and security of home.

At one point during those months, Lavinia visited Syracuse, New York. Years later, she recalled visiting the courthouse jail. How cruel it was, she thought, to lock people away in cells. The prisoners treated her with interest and spoke to her with kindness. She felt sympathy for them and throughout her life was convinced that "we can do better and eliminate causes [of crime]."

Family was important to Lavinia. Pictured from left to right are Lavinia, her sister Caroline Delia, her mother, and Minnie.

Moving onto the World Stage

During the summer of 1862, P. T. Barnum, the famous showman, sent an agent to Middleborough to interview Lavinia. Barnum had read several press reports about her success on the riverboat. When the agent confirmed the reports, Barnum sent him back to Middleborough to offer Lavinia a job. Would she consider appearing as a curiosity at Barnum's American Museum in New York City? Barnum promised that she would be an even bigger success in New York than she had been on the Floating Palace. He offered a tour of Europe as an added incentive.

Lavinia's immediate response was no. If anyone should profit from her fame, she felt it should be Colonel Wood. After all, he had introduced her to show business and returned her safely home. However, he never sent an offer. As much as Lavinia wanted to see more of the world, she steadfastly refused to accept Barnum's offer.

Her parents had other concerns. Barnum was known as the "Prince of Humbugs." He had spent a lifetime fooling the public. It seemed as if P. T. Barnum would do anything to make a dollar. The Bumps feared that if Lavinia accepted Barnum's offer, she would become another of his humbugs.

HUMBUG!

A humbug is a fraud, a hoax, or a deception; something that is not what it pretends to be.

BARNUM

Phineas Taylor Barnum was born on July 5, 1810, and raised in Bethel, Connecticut. In 1834, at age 24, he moved to New York City. In those days, New York was a center for hoaxes and deceptions. Newspapers carried stories that were clearly fakes. Fooling the public made many wealthy, and P. T. Barnum did not want to be left out.

In 1835 he purchased a slave named Joice Heth for $1,000 (about $27,000 in today's dollars). At the time, Barnum had no qualms about becoming a slave owner. He

This photo of P. T. Barnum was taken about the time Lavinia first met him.

was eager to earn a living by whatever means possible, and he was convinced that Heth would attract a crowd. Her previous owner claimed that Heth was 161 years old and had taken care of the infant George Washington. Barnum knew that such a fantastic claim would capture the public's curiosity.

He was right. Heth's age, her color, and her connection to Washington made her a genuine curiosity. People flocked to see her. Heth told stories about "little George." She sang hymns and answered questions.

When the crowds began to wither away, Barnum pulled an even greater hoax. He wrote an anonymous letter to a newspaper claiming that Heth was a fake. She wasn't even a person, the letter said, but an automaton, or machine, made of whalebone, rubber, and springs. He signed the letter, "A Visitor." This letter attracted bigger crowds. People wanted to see for themselves whether Heth was human or mechanical.

Barnum believed that humbugs and fakes were as profitable as genuine curiosities. People enjoyed the chance to decide for themselves. When a visitor asked Barnum, "Is it real or is it humbug?" Barnum replied, "Persons who pay their money at the door have the right to form their own opinions after they have got upstairs." In other words, anyone who buys a ticket is welcome to make up his or her own mind.

BARNUM'S AMERICAN MUSEUM

In 1841, Barnum opened his American Museum on the corner of Broadway and Ann Street in New York City. (This is where he wanted Lavinia to perform.) The museum grew quickly thanks to Barnum's advertising skill. He placed ads in all the New York papers, mounted large posters between the windows of the museum, and used whatever schemes he could devise to snag customers.

Barnum's American Museum was the most famous showplace of its day. Unlike many theaters or museums, the American Museum provided exhibits and entertainments suitable for families. Men, women, and children, rich and poor, native-born and immigrants all flocked to the museum to see Barnum's latest exhibits. Live entertainers sang, danced, and played musical instruments. Actors and actresses put on plays in the theater. Exhibit halls were devoted to birds, fish, and mammals. Some of these animals were alive; others were stuffed.

The American Museum is seen at the far left of this 1855 print of New York City. Barnum claimed that as many as 15,000 people per day paid a quarter (about $6.50 today) to visit his museum. Children paid half price.

Dioramas showed scenes of Paris, Jerusalem, and Dublin. One of Barnum's humbugs was his claim that he had imported at great expense a working model of Niagara Falls. People rushed to see it. What they found was an 18-inch-tall model of the falls. It was a working model, but it certainly wasn't anything like the real Niagara Falls.

Children made up about one-third of the US population during the 1860s. Many of Barnum's exhibits were expressly designed to interest children. Barnum offered half-price tickets for children and special afternoon showings. Patriotic programs, as well as religious and educational ones, convinced parents to bring children to the museum. Over the years, he added strolling musicians, live animals, mechanical figures, and displays especially designed to entertain children. He wrote, "There was no picture so beautiful as ten thousand smiling, bright-eyed, happy children, and no music as sweet as their clear ringing laughter."

Gradually, the educational exhibits were replaced with more entertaining ones. Barnum hired American Indians to demonstrate war dances. Jugglers, gymnasts, and magicians performed feats of skill. He wanted to give the public "abundant and wholesome attractions for a small sum of money." Barnum didn't hesitate to provide "curiosities" if they helped attract crowds. For example, Mr. Nellis, a man born without arms, amazed audiences with his ability to load a gun, cut paper airplanes, and play musical instruments with his feet.

Barnum later said, "Now and then some one would call out 'humbug' or 'charlatan,' but so much the better for me. It helped to advertise me, and I was willing to bear the reputation—and I engaged queer curiosities, and even monstrosities, simply to add to the notoriety of the Museum."

Museums like Barnum's were limited to bigger cities like New York, Boston, and Philadelphia. Children in towns and villages attended county agricultural fairs and special events like hot-air balloon liftoffs. Touring shows often brought curiosities to smaller towns, although showboats stopped traveling the rivers during wartime.

During the 1860s, with the nation at war, Barnum began playing to his customers' patriotism. As the war progressed, he created war-related exhibits, displaying items recovered from Fort Sumter, a set of slave chains and shackles, and a Confederate flag. One of Barnum's popular actresses, Dora Dawson, appeared draped in a Union flag. War heroes, like 12-year-old drummer boy Robert Henry Hendershot, appeared on Barnum's stage. Hendershot had been playing his drum on the battlefield at Fredericksburg, Virginia, when a Confederate shell struck and shattered the drum. The young drummer grabbed a musket and took a Confederate soldier captive. Barnum knew that such bravery would inspire audiences at the museum, and it did.

One young man, a frequent visitor to the museum, later wrote that Barnum himself would often come out from behind the ticket booth and shake the hands of his visitors.

A MOMENTOUS DECISION

When Barnum had an idea, he didn't give up easily. He wanted Lavinia Warren for his museum. When his agent reported Lavinia's response, Barnum came up with a plan. He sent an invitation to Lavinia and her parents to visit him at his Bridgeport, Connecticut, home. They did so. Barnum offered Lavinia $10 a week plus expenses (equal to about $250 today). It was far more money than she would have earned as a schoolteacher or on the showboat.

Much to Lavinia's surprise, her parents supported Barnum's plan. He proposed that she appear at the American Museum in New York followed immediately by a European tour. Lavinia's sense of adventure and desire to see Europe clinched the deal. She agreed to sign with Barnum. Looking back on that moment, Lavinia wrote, "I little thought when we accepted that invitation how many important events would quickly follow and be crowded into my life's history."

Lavinia moved into the New York City home of one of Barnum's daughters. Barnum spared no expense on his new employee. He hired a seamstress to sew several beautiful gowns for her. Some cost nearly $2,000. He selected exquisite jewelry to match. When all was ready, Barnum moved Lavinia to New York's St. Nicholas Hotel. He wanted to introduce his newest marvel to the world in one of the city's most marvelous hotels.

The St. Nicholas was elegant and luxurious. It was the first New York City hotel that cost over $1 million to build. Unlike many homes or other hotels, it had central heating, as well as a fireplace in every room. The hotel opened in 1853 with 200 guest rooms. Most American homes did not have indoor plumbing or flush toilets until about 1870, but every room at the St. Nicolas had hot and cold running water, as well as a bath and toilet. Barnum sent invitations to New York newspapers inviting reporters to come to the St. Nicholas to meet Lavinia. Many wrote flattering articles in their papers. After a December 23, 1862, meeting, a reporter for the *New York Tribune* wrote:

> Yesterday we saw a very pretty and intelligent little lady at the St. Nicholas Hotel, in this city. This woman in miniature is 21 years of age, weighs 29 pounds, and measures 32 inches in height. . . She moves about the drawing room with the grace and dignity of a queen, and yet she is entirely devoid of affectation [phoniness], is modest and lady–like in her deportment.

The *New York Sun* of December 23, 1862, reported, "Her dresses are magnificent, being clothed at the rate of $2000 per outfit, and sparkling with jewels and splendor. Many would deem it a show to see the dresses, but dresses and contents together are a little ahead of anything which tiny hoops have enclosed for many a year."

Years later, Lavinia pasted clippings of the articles into her memoir. She was careful to note, "I disclaim all vanity in offering to my readers these 'opinions' so flattering in their tone. If nature endowed me with any superior personal attraction, it was comparatively small compensation for the inconvenience, trouble, and annoyance imposed upon me by my diminutive stature." It is one of the few times that Lavinia mentions the problems she faced living in a world designed for taller people. In fact, her autobiography, written when she was in her 60s, contains relatively few comments about her size or the inconveniences of life as a little person. Outwardly, she appeared cheerful and able to face whatever life sent her way.

A CHANGE OF PLANS

The glowing newspaper reports and Lavinia's public success thrilled Barnum. Ticket sales soared. Lavinia attracted bigger crowds than even Barnum had expected. He asked her to remain at the museum for a few more weeks. He even offered her $1,000 per week if she would postpone the European trip.

Lavinia declined. She was eager to go to Europe. The same sense of adventure that led her to accept Colonel Woods's offer to join his showboat had persuaded her to accept Barnum's contract, and he had promised that her first public appearance would be in England. Lavinia was fascinated with a world she had only read about. She immediately wrote to Barnum:

St. Nicholas Hotel, Dec. 26, 1862
P. T. Barnum, Esq. Dear Sir,

In reply to your note of this morning, I beg to say that in consequence of Messrs. Ball & Black not being able

to complete all the jewels ordered for me, my departure
for London will be delayed a week or two. I [will], how–
ever, visit Boston, as arranged, tomorrow and as I do
not contemplate giving public exhibitions, until I have
appeared, as per contract, before the Courts of Europe, I
must respectfully decline your offer.

Your obedient Servant,
Lavinia Warren

A two-week wait for the jewelry was all right, and a
trip to Boston would do, but Lavinia did not intend to
remain in New York after that. She left immediately for
Massachusetts. She hosted two receptions for wealthy
Bostonians at the city's famous Parker House Hotel and
spent an entire day with Massachusetts governor John
Albion Andrew.

Lavinia may have convinced herself that her letter
to Barnum ended any discussion about staying in New
York, but Barnum was not so easily dismissed. While
Lavinia was traveling to Boston, Barnum went to Middleborough to meet with her parents. Persuasive as
always, he convinced the Bumps that Lavinia must delay
the European tour. The Bumps didn't argue. After all,
what did a few weeks matter when Barnum was willing
to pay their daughter so generously? Lavinia's mother
hustled off to Boston to talk some sense into her stub-
born daughter.

As it happened, Tom Thumb, a famous Barnum
dwarf, was in Boston at the same time. That's when he

JOHN ALBION ANDREW

John Albion Andrew had been elected governor in 1860. Sensing that war would soon begin between Northern and Southern states, he had requested funds from the Massachusetts Legislature to support the state militia. When the first shots were fired on Fort Sumter, the Massachusetts Sixth regiment was the first to reach Washington. Governor Andrew took his support a step further when he organized the 54th Massachusetts Regiment. It was the nation's first military unit consisting entirely of black soldiers. Many white Americans doubted the character and ability of African Americans. Governor Andrew had no such doubts. He said that his reputation would depend on "the rise and fall in history of the 54th Massachusetts Regiment." The 54th fought with courage in battle. By the war's end, nearly 200,000 black soldiers and sailors served in Union forces.

got his first glimpse of Lavinia. According to Barnum's later recollections, as well as to reports in several newspapers, Tom fell in love at first sight.

Lavinia was with her mother at the time, and Huldah did not hesitate to say that she was unimpressed with the famous Tom Thumb. In fact, she said, he was too proud and aristocratic to suit her. She didn't like his mustache, either.

Lavinia's response was more reserved. Many years later, she said simply, "I had heard of General Tom Thumb and seen him once, but knew nothing of his character, reputation, and fame." Whatever Lavinia felt after that first meeting in Boston, she kept to herself. She was soon to see more, much more, of the famous Tom Thumb.

5

CHARLEY

Lavinia was fully aware that she was not the first little person to work for Barnum. That honor had gone to Tom Thumb. Tom Thumb was the stage name of Charles Sherwood Stratton, the youngest child of Sherwood and Cynthia Stratton. He was born on January 4, 1838, in Bridgeport, Connecticut.

Charley was a big baby. He weighed nine and a half pounds at birth, but he stopped growing when he was about 18 months old. Charley, like Lavinia, was a proportionate dwarf. However, while Lavinia's family accepted her as she was, Charley's family was embarrassed by his size. The Strattons already had two average-sized daughters. What was wrong with Charley? The father could not imagine what the future held for his tiny son. How would he make a living? How would he survive in a world too big for him?

The solution came in a visit from P. T. Barnum in November 1842. Barnum had stopped in Bridgeport to visit his brother, Philo. Philo told him about the tiny boy who lived nearby, and Barnum immediately went to the Stratton home to meet young Charley. He later wrote, "He was the smallest child I had ever seen who could

In this famous photo, a very young Tom Thumb leans on his mentor, P. T. Barnum.

walk alone. He was not two feet in height and weighed less than sixteen pounds, a bright-eyed little fellow, with light hair and ruddy cheeks." Barnum went on to say that Charley was "exceedingly bashful, but after some coaxing he was induced to converse with me." It was the beginning of a long relationship that brought fame and fortune to them both.

Barnum offered the boy's parents three dollars a week if they would allow him to exhibit four-year-old Charley for a month at the American Museum in New York. In addition, Barnum promised to pay all expenses. Charley's father readily agreed. For the cash-poor Strattons, three dollars a week (about $75.00 today) seemed like a fortune. The possibility of Charley's fame and fortune was a tempting solution to their problems.

Charley and his mother traveled to New York and stayed in a room on the fifth floor of the American Museum. Barnum began working with Charley. He taught him proper manners and helped him memorize scripts for several small scenes. Barnum taught Charley to sing, dance, and act. Charley was a natural mimic who learned his parts easily even though there were many parts to learn.

Barnum designed various roles for Charley to perform in his stage acts. He would pretend to be Cupid, Hercules, Napoleon, and various other characters from history and mythology. He dressed to fit the roles. Barnum practiced with Charley until the boy had his roles down perfectly.

ADVERTISING CHARLEY

Barnum wanted to create buzz about his newest exhibit, so he renamed Charley "Tom Thumb" after a character in an English fairy tale. Barnum feared that if he told people that Charley, now called Tom Thumb, was only four years old, they would assume he would soon grow bigger. Consequently, he told the public that Charley was an 11-year-old British boy. Why British? Barnum had noticed that Americans were impressed by anything and everything from Europe. Barnum claimed that Charley had recently arrived from England.

THE ORIGINAL TOM THUMB

"Tom Thumb," a British fairy tale written in the 1600s, is about a boy who is only as big as his mother's thumb. The tiny boy is nearly eaten after he falls into his mother's pie. After several other narrow escapes, he returns home to live happily ever after.

Charley's mother was unaware of the deception until she arrived in New York. She was shocked and angry to see the advertisements. It was too late to back out, but she didn't forgive Barnum until Tom Thumb proved so successful that Barnum extended Charley's contract.

Barnum used other stunts to introduce Charley to New Yorkers. He barged into the homes of New York's leading newspaper editors at dinnertime and placed Charley on the dinner table, where he danced and sang for the editors and their families. The children laughed, which delighted their parents. By the time Tom Thumb appeared at the American Museum, newspaper editors had published glowing accounts.

BARNUM'S GREATEST SUCCESS

Crowds rushed to see Barnum's latest wonder. Audiences agreed that Tom Thumb was funny, talented, and cute. The show was appropriate for families, which was unusual in the 1840s. In earlier days, respectable people and children did not go to museums or theaters because they believed the shows weren't fit for women and children. Barnum helped change American entertainment.

Once Tom was a proven success, Barnum increased his weekly pay. He gave Charley's dad a well-paying job as an assistant and began using Tom to promote other exhibits. Tom performed at the American Museum for several weeks. Then Barnum sent him to perform in other US cities and towns under the care of his parents and one of Barnum's managers.

Life was not easy for young Charley Stratton. He not only faced the problem of being much smaller than others his age but also was forced to grow up quickly. He drank wine with meals when he was five and smoked cigars by age seven. He spent most of his time with adults and rarely played with children his own age. What age was he anyway? Barnum had convinced the public that Charley was seven years older than the date on his birth certificate. He was expected to act much older than he really was.

Lavinia and Charley had more in common than their size. Like Lavinia, Charley was a trickster who loved to laugh. He set traps for Barnum by stringing twine or wire in doorways or across hallways. When Barnum pretended to trip, Charley roared with laughter. Barnum liked children and did his best to care for Charley. He read him storybooks, something Charley's illiterate parents were unable to do, and he carried Charley from place to place. Given Charley's small size, walking great distances was difficult, if not impossible.

CHARLEY TOURS THE WORLD

Charley was only six years old in January 1844 when Barnum took him and his parents to Europe for the first time. As always, Barnum set his sights high. He wanted to present Tom Thumb to Great Britain's Queen Victoria. At first, that didn't seem likely, but Barnum was not one to give up. Tom performed at the Princess's Theater in London to huge success. Barnum moved him to a larger venue, Egyptian Hall. Finally, after several weeks in London, Barnum received an invitation to bring Tom Thumb to the queen's residence at Buckingham Palace.

Charley was no longer shy. He made a graceful bow before the queen and said, "Good evening, Ladies and Gentlemen!" The queen took his hand in hers, walked him around her gallery, and asked him questions. His answers caused everyone present to join in friendly laughter. The comments in her diary show her to be a careful observer and more sensitive to the little boy's needs than many others were. She wrote:

> After dinner we saw the greatest curiosity I, or indeed anybody, ever saw, viz: a little dwarf, only 25 inches high & 15 lbs. in weight. No description can give an idea of this little creature, whose name was Charles Stratton, born they say in 32, which makes him 12 years old. He is American, and gave us his card, with Gen. Tom Thumb written on it. . . . One cannot help feeling sorry for the poor little thing & wishing he could be properly cared for. The people who show him off tease him a good deal.

As her diary entry shows, even the queen had been deceived about Charley's real age. Imagine how her sympathy would have increased had she known he was only six years old, not 12.

The queen invited Charley to Buckingham Palace on three separate occasions. The royal family gave him expensive gifts, including a miniature gold watch and a tiny card case decorated with gold and precious jewels. Perhaps even more valuable was the queen's goodwill. Once the British people heard that Tom Thumb had charmed Queen Victoria, they wanted to meet him too. Ticket sales for Tom Thumb's performances reached $500 a day.

In this sketch, Barnum helps a young Charles Stratton prepare for one of his many roles.

To keep Tom Thumb in the news, Barnum ordered a specially made miniature carriage. A team of four ponies pulled it through the streets of London. It was a great advertisement for Tom's stage performances.

Charley spent three years in Europe under Barnum's supervision. His parents went along. The group toured major cities in England, Scotland, and Ireland. Charley went to Paris and appeared before the French king, Louis Philippe, who gave Charley an emerald-and-diamond pin. Charley visited Belgium too, and in Spain he performed for Queen Isabella.

BACK IN THE UNITED STATES

By the time Charley returned to New York, he was a self-confident performer and an experienced traveler. He was also rich, and he wasn't yet 10 years old! Charley worked hard for his money. For example, Barnum's advertisement in the *New York Daily Tribune* of March 4, 1847, promised four performances by Tom Thumb at 11:00 AM, 3:00 PM, 7:00 PM, and finally at 8:00 PM. It was a grueling schedule. The ad claimed that Tom Thumb had appeared before all the crowned heads of Europe and had been seen by five million people.

After performing for four weeks at the American Museum, Charley returned home to Bridgeport. Now that he was world-famous, everyone in Bridgeport wanted to meet the hometown hero. Charley spent his first two days giving performances in Bridgeport. People who had known him as a young boy were surprised by how different he seemed. He was no bigger, but he appeared older and wiser. One man said that Charley had been "Barnumized."

Now that Tom Thumb had proved his value, Barnum rewrote his contract. Sherwood Stratton, Charley's father, and Barnum would split equally any money that Charley earned as Tom Thumb. Some was put aside for Charley's future. His parents used part of the earnings to build a new family home in Bridgeport. The rooms set aside for Charley were built to meet his needs, with lower shelves, smaller furniture, and so on. Charley spent a month at home with his family before going back on tour.

In April 1847, Charley and his parents left for Washington, DC. Barnum traveled with them. They visited the White House and met President James Polk (1845–1849). From there they traveled to Richmond, Virginia. They circled back through New England, visiting Lowell and Boston in Massachusetts and Providence, Rhode Island. They stopped at many smaller towns and cities along the way. They then traveled west through northern New York, stopping at Troy, Albany, Buffalo, Niagara Falls, and other towns. They returned to Connecticut in the fall.

Did all this travel tire Charley out, or did he enjoy it? Barnum doesn't say, and since Charley never wrote an autobiography, we have no way to know. In later years, however, he confided to Lavinia, "You know, I never had much childhood. Mr. Barnum took me when I was four, and trained me to speak and act like a man."

READY TO SETTLE DOWN

———◇———

Tom Thumb spent the next several years on tour. He visited the nation of Cuba, traveled throughout the United States, and returned to Europe with Barnum in 1857. By then, Charley was 19 years old. He had grown a few inches in his late teens. At age 18, he was 35 inches tall, but the added height didn't dim the enthusiasm of his fans. After visiting London and Paris, Charley performed before Dutch and German audiences. Barnum did not stay with Charley the entire time now that Charley was old enough to travel on his own. He hired various assistants to provide help when needed.

When Charley finally returned to America, he was a wealthy young man. He built a home for himself in Bridgeport. He bought ponies, which he enjoyed racing, and a yacht, the *Maggie B*, to sail on Long Island Sound.

But Charley felt that something was missing. He wanted to find a wife to share his good fortune. He knew he had found her when he first saw Lavinia in Boston during the fall of 1862. It was pure coincidence that he happened to be there at the exact time that Lavinia appeared. She may not have taken much notice of the famous Tom Thumb, but he had certainly noticed her.

6

Friends or Lovers?

In late December, Lavinia returned to New York to appear at the American Museum as Barnum and her parents wanted. She took rooms at the Fifth Avenue Hotel. On January 1, 1863, she began receiving visitors there.

On the same day, Abraham Lincoln issued the Emancipation Proclamation. Lavinia made no mention of the proclamation in her autobiography, but she noted that she met many important Civil War generals during her early days in New York. "I remember myself looking on them as they came before me in full uniform as something quite apart from ordinary life, though I little dreamed how long the terrible war would last or how rapidly these smiling gentlemen were making history." The war had been raging for almost two years, and although no one knew it at the time, fighting would continue for at least two more.

At first, Lavinia met people privately in receptions called levees. Her intelligence and quick wit made her a good conversationalist. She also sang in a high, sweet voice.

General Winfield Scott was staying at the same hotel as Lavinia. He invited her to visit him in his room because he was too ill to attend one of her levees. Scott was a national hero. He first earned fame in the War of 1812 and later led the forceful removal of the Cherokee Indians from their lands in Georgia. More than 4,000 of the 15,000 Cherokees died, but at the time this tragic event, now called the Trail of Tears, did not diminish Scott's reputation. He was a hero in the Mexican-American War too. On September 14, 1847, he had led the capture of Mexico City. By the time Lavinia met him in New York, he had gained the rank of brevet lieutenant general, the same rank granted to George Washington.

General Scott took Lavinia's hand and drew her close. She looked up at him in amazement. She never imagined that such an important man would want to spend time with her. Lavinia considered General Scott to be nearly as great as Washington.

Despite Scott's high rank and past glories, President Lincoln chose a younger man to lead the Union troops in the Civil War: General George B. McClellan. McClellan was a popular general, although he was not nearly as aggressive as Lincoln would have liked. In fact, after the

Union defeat at Manassas, Virginia, Lincoln removed McClellan as general in chief and gave him charge of the Army of the Potomac. However, when McClellan failed to follow Confederate commander Robert E. Lee's troops after the Union defeat at Antietam, Maryland, Lincoln demoted McClellan again. He replaced him with General Ambrose Burnside.

Lavinia met both McClellan and Burnside at her levees in New York over the 1863 New Year's holiday. Burnside and his Army of the Potomac had just suffered a staggering defeat at Fredericksburg. Nearly 13,300 Union soldiers died. Confederate losses totaled 4,500 men. Robert E. Lee reportedly said, "It is well that war is so terrible, or we should grow too fond of it."

Later that year, Lincoln would transfer Burnside to Ohio. He dealt with troublemakers there and led campaigns into Kentucky and eastern Tennessee. Eventually, Burnside returned to Virginia to lead Union troops there. Although Lavinia did not mention Burnside's appearance, many others did. His beard extended from his ears down his cheeks and up over his mouth, ending in a mustache. The word *sideburns* was created from his last name to describe his unique facial hair.

Thanks to Barnum, the American Museum attracted many of New York City's rich and famous citizens. Lavinia met people like Cornelius Vanderbilt and John Jacob Astor, who were among the wealthiest businessmen in America. They brought their families and Barnum arranged for them to meet Lavinia in private. It seemed as if everyone wanted to see Barnum's newest sensation.

Although Lavinia was considered a curiosity, there was nothing freakish about her. Barnum promoted her by saying, "Her size is that of a child, her language that of an adult." Even so, Lavinia's "cuteness" attracted large crowds. Many people reacted as Stephen Douglas had. They had trouble thinking of Lavinia as an adult with adult cares and concerns. It was a constant source of irritation to her.

CHARLEY CONFESSES

On January 2, 1863, Lavinia began appearing at Barnum's American Museum. One day Charley Stratton stopped by the museum to visit with Barnum. Charley was no longer under contract to Barnum, but their friendship continued. After watching Lavinia at the museum, Charley asked for a private meeting with Barnum. Barnum later wrote that Charley inquired about Lavinia, and then said with great feeling, "Mr. Barnum, that is the most charming little lady I ever saw, and I believe she was created on purpose to be my wife! I want to marry and settle down in life, and I really feel as if I must marry that young lady."

In later recollections, Barnum reported that Charley's infatuation with Lavinia had begun even earlier, during their brief meeting in Boston. Charley began traveling

Newspapers published drawings like this of Charley and Lavinia walking along New York City streets.

to New York City to visit his married sister. His mother expressed surprise. After all, Charley had never shown such interest in his sister and her family. Soon, however, it became clear that it was not his sister who interested him.

It became a nightly routine for Charley to escort Lavinia home from the museum after her performances. She seemed to enjoy his company. As an 1874 pamphlet about the couple noted, "Miss Warren, who dislikes affectation, and who is as truthful as she is fascinating, did not discourage the attention of her lover. She acknowledged that his society was very agreeable to her, and that his absence was to her a source of pain."

Charley's devotion did not go unnoticed. After all, it was impossible for either of the little people to go anywhere in public without attracting attention. Newspaper reporters were always looking for a good story.

NUTT MOVES IN

Public notice was not the only problem the couple faced. A bigger challenge came from another little person named Commodore Nutt. George Washington Morrison Nutt had begun working at the American Museum in 1860. At first, George played the role of Civil War drummer boy, but Barnum soon made a switch. He gave George the title of commodore even though it was obvious that Nutt was not a high-ranking navy officer. He was a 16-year-old New Hampshire farm boy who was only 29 inches tall, six inches shorter than Tom Thumb. Barnum believed that military titles added to the entertainment value of the little men. He referred to Charley as General Tom Thumb.

Like Charley, George had a quick wit and enjoyed performing. Barnum hoped that George would become the new Tom Thumb and would generate the same kind of excitement. Barnum had offered George a three-year contract at $30,000 plus all expenses. As a result, the newspapers dubbed him the "$30,000 Nutt."

Commodore Nutt looked like a younger version of Tom Thumb. Many museum visitors thought Barnum had merely changed Tom Thumb's name to Commodore Nutt. At the time that Nutt first appeared at the American Museum, Tom Thumb was on tour under his own management. Barnum convinced him to return to New York and appear side-by-side with George. Charley had gained considerable weight by this time and was much larger than the slender George. Even after the two men appeared together, many people continued to believe that Barnum was pulling another hoax.

In 1862, Barnum arranged for Commodore Nutt to go to Washington, DC. Barnum met

Commodore Nutt, like Tom Thumb, often appeared in military uniform.

him there. In his autobiography, Barnum recalled that meeting:

> I received an invitation from President Lincoln to call at the White House with my little friend. Arriving at the appointed hour, I was informed that the President was in a special meeting, but that he had left word if I called to be shown in to him with the Commodore. These were dark days in the rebellion and I felt that my visit, if not ill timed, must at all events be brief. When we were admitted, Mr. Lincoln received us cordially, and introduced us to the members of the Cabinet, . . . President Lincoln bent down his long, lank body, and taking Nutt by the hand he said, "Commodore, permit me to give you a parting word of advice. When you are in command of your fleet, if you find yourself in danger of being taken prisoner, I advise you to wade ashore."
>
> The Commodore found the laugh against him, but placing himself at the side of the President, and gradually raising his eyes up the whole length of Mr. Lincoln's very long legs, he replied, "I guess, Mr. President, you could do that better than I could."

George was two years younger than Lavinia, but the difference in their ages did not stop him from thinking that he could win her heart. She thought of him as a boy, a younger friend perhaps, but not a lover. Although George never hid his attraction to Lavinia, he had no idea that Charley was contemplating marriage.

THE PROPOSAL

——•◇•——

According to Barnum, Charley spent as much time as possible with Lavinia, and then he told Barnum of his intentions. When he confided to Barnum that he planned to marry Lavinia, Barnum replied that she was already engaged.

Charley was shocked. "To whom?" he asked. "To Commodore Nutt?"

"No," Barnum replied. "To me."

Charley immediately recognized it for the joke that it was. He laughed. "Never mind. You may exhibit her for a while but I do hope you will favor my suit."

Charley asked Barnum's help. If Barnum would invite Lavinia to his Bridgeport home for the weekend, Charley would meet them there. He would show Lavinia the properties he owned, which he hoped would impress her. Bridgeport, as opposed to New York City, would provide at least a small measure of privacy for the actual proposal.

Charley met Lavinia and Barnum at the Bridgeport train station in one of his miniature carriages. His coachman was decked out in full uniform, including a hat with a velvet ribbon and silver buckle. Charley left no detail to chance. He escorted Lavinia to Barnum's elegant home, Lindencroft.

After Lavinia had a brief rest at Lindencroft, Charley took her for a carriage ride past his parents' house. He showed her the miniature apartment his father had built especially for him. He drove her past several other properties he owned before taking her back to Barnum's home.

On their return, Barnum asked Lavinia how she enjoyed her ride.

"It was very pleasant," she said. "But it seems as if you and Tom Thumb own all of Bridgeport."

Later in the day, Charley brought his mother to Lindencroft for dinner. She met Lavinia and returned home after the meal. Barnum retired for the evening, leaving Charley and Lavinia alone. They played backgammon, a popular board game. As Charley later told Barnum, he asked Lavinia about her upcoming trip to Europe and shared his own experiences overseas.

Lavinia's excitement about the trip was obvious. She trusted Barnum to provide for her needs and to arrange visits with all the kings and queens of Europe. When Charley asked if she would be lonely, she told him that she was not going alone. Barnum and several others would accompany her.

"I wish I were going over, for I know all about the different countries and could explain them to you," Charley said. Lavinia seemed to encourage the idea, and finally Charley said, "Don't you think it would be pleasanter if we went as man and wife?"

Lavinia appeared surprised at the proposal, but when Charley assured her that he was serious, she readily agreed—if her mother approved.

At that very moment, someone knocked at the door.

Commodore Nutt had arrived to spend the weekend. Neither Charley nor Lavinia said a word to George about the proposal. They knew the news would crush him. Lavinia went off to bed. So did the Commodore.

But Charley stayed up, and once quiet had settled over the house, he knocked on Barnum's bedroom door. Barnum was awake and seemed to be waiting for news.

"We are engaged!" Charley announced with great joy. "We are engaged!"

Charley and Lavinia kept their engagement a secret for several days. In the meantime, Charley sent a letter to Lavinia's mother to ask for her blessing on the marriage. At first, she hesitated. Was it his mustache? If so, Charley promised to shave it off.

But it wasn't the mustache that she feared. Was this another scheme of Barnum's? Barnum himself assured her that he would immediately cancel his contract with Lavinia when she married. Only then did Huldah consent to the marriage.

Meanwhile, Charley felt that someone should tell George about the engagement. He asked Barnum to do so, but Barnum replied, "Do it yourself, General."

Lavinia stepped forward. "I will do it," she said, and arranged for Barnum to call Commodore Nutt to his office. Together Barnum and Lavinia broke the news. George turned pale, according to Barnum's account, choked a bit, and said, "I hope you may be happy." He whirled around and left the room.

THE BIGGEST LITTLE WEDDING

When the engagement was finally announced to the world, it was front-page news. Long articles provided brief biographies of the bride and groom, an account of their meeting and courtship, and details about the upcoming wedding. In Massachusetts, the *Middleborough Gazette* reported on January 17, 1863, "The New York papers are filled with the particulars of this most extraordinary love affair among the little folks." But it wasn't only big city papers that carried the news. On February 25, 1863, the *Goodhue Volunteer*, a newspaper in the small town of Red Wing, Minnesota, reported with enthusiasm, "Miss Lavinia Warren's fingers are all Thumb's."

Newspaper stories about the upcoming wedding brought more and more people to see Lavinia at the American Museum. In fact, so many people flocked to the museum to see her that ticket sales frequently passed

This is one of the *cartes de visite* sold during Lavinia's engagement to Charley.

$3,000 per day. Barnum reported that Lavinia sold more than $300 worth of her photographs each day. That's close to $6,000 in today's dollars. Barnum hired Charley to assist with the sales of the photos, which were called *cartes de visite*. While some were of Lavinia alone, many included Tom Thumb as well.

"NOT FOR FIFTY THOUSAND DOLLARS"

When Barnum learned that Lavinia had a 14-year-old sister, Minnie, who was extremely attractive and even smaller than Lavinia, he hatched another plan. If he could get Minnie and Commodore Nutt to join Charley and

CARTES DE VISITE

Beginning in about 1857, photographers made small photos mounted on heavy-duty card stock for entertainers as a form of advertising. These *cartes de visite* were popular souvenirs. They measured 2½ inches by 4 inches. During the Civil War, many families posed for such photos before a son or husband went off to war. All too often, it was the last photograph of the young soldier. *Cartes de visite*, also called card portraits, were relatively inexpensive and were popular not only in the United States but also throughout the world.

Lavinia on stage, he would have "a quartette of the most wonderful, intelligent and perfectly formed ladies and gentlemen in miniature the world ever produced." It did not happen right away. Eventually, however, the four did travel the world together, thrilling audiences everywhere.

Even without Minnie, Barnum knew that he had discovered gold in Lavinia. Business was booming. As Barnum said, "I could afford to give them a fine wedding, and I did so." But he was in no hurry to do it. A long engagement would be good for business. He offered Charley and Lavinia $15,000 to delay the wedding for a month while they continued their exhibitions at the museum.

"Not for fifty thousand dollars," Charley reportedly said, and Lavinia chimed in, "Good for you, Charley, only you ought to have said not for a hundred thousand, for I would not."

In her autobiography, Lavinia speaks more bluntly. She writes, "As the General and myself were expected to marry each other and not Mr. Barnum, and as moreover we were neither of us marrying for money, we didn't quite see that a money offer was any part of the business, so we declined."

Despite reports in the press that Barnum was staging the wedding as a show, no tickets were sold. The wedding would take place in a church, not a concert hall, and it was to be presided over by a clergyman. As Lavinia wrote, "Everybody in the church came by invitation, and thus the ceremony was conducted as would be any marriage of people less before the public."

In terms of the actual ceremony, Lavinia spoke the truth. But no other 19th-century wedding caused such a commotion and aroused such public interest as the wedding of Tom Thumb and Lavinia Warren.

Barnum's next proposal was of a more romantic nature. He wanted them to marry on February 14, Valentine's Day. Again, Charley and Lavinia refused. They set the date for February 10, 1863, a Tuesday, at noon.

A BARNUM PRODUCTION

—◇—

Charley and Lavinia allowed Barnum to take charge of the wedding. After all, Barnum had experience planning big events. He respected the wishes of the bride and groom and treated the wedding as a solemn occasion.

At first, Charley and Lavinia planned to have a small, private wedding, but the public protested. Everyone, it seemed, wanted to share in the celebration. Charley and Lavinia finally agreed to a large church wedding. The first church they chose, Trinity Chapel in New York City, turned them down. The rector feared that there would be too much publicity surrounding the wedding. Next, they asked if Grace Church at 802 Broadway would allow the wedding to take place there. Grace Church welcomed them, but even after the church's minister, the Reverend Dr. Taylor, gave his approval, controversy erupted. Many people assumed that the wedding was another of Barnum's hoaxes.

Charley and Lavinia did everything in their power to convince the public that this was no hoax. They denied rumors that they had been turned down by numerous churches. Instead, they composed a public notice published in the *New York Commercial Advertiser*:

One thing is certain, if we both live and have our health, we shall be married at 12 o'clock on Tuesday, the 10th day of February, proximo [next month], and the ceremonies will be conducted strictly as heretofore announced.

Jan. 24th.   Charles S. Stratton.

Lavinia Warren.

There's no doubt that Barnum benefited from the publicity surrounding the wedding. Not only were Lavinia's levees at the museum filled to overflowing, but also sales of *cartes de visite* had increased dramatically. Crowds stayed to visit the museum's other exhibits, thereby adding more than a few pennies to Barnum's already overstuffed pockets.

GUESTS AND GIFTS

Lavinia did not want her wedding to become a theatrical event. It was her wedding, and she intended it to be a dignified religious ceremony. Even when people offered Barnum more than $75 (nearly $1,300 in today's dollars) for an invitation to the wedding, he replied that invitations were not for sale.

Barnum printed the 2,000 invitations on heavy card stock. Each invitation contained a ticket that admitted the bearer to the wedding and reception. Charley's private secretary signed each ticket. There were also two calling cards—one belonging to the bride and one to the groom—neatly tied together with ribbons.

The bride and groom's family and friends were at the top of the invitation list. Barnum carefully chose the other guests. He sent invitations to the elite of New York City society: newspaper editors, business leaders, bankers, and lawyers. He invited the governors of several states and their wives. Herman Melville, author of the great American novel *Moby Dick*, published in 1851, received an invitation. So did several members of Congress, Union generals, and President and Mrs. Lincoln.

The rich and famous sent exquisite gifts. Few were useful despite their expense. Gifts included a miniature silver tea set, a miniature silver horse and chariot (the horse's eyes were garnets), a set of silver coffee spoons lined with gold, and many items of jewelry. The Lincolns, who did not attend the wedding, sent a set of Chinese fire screens inlaid with gold, silver, and pearl.

Barnum gave Lavinia and Charley several expensive gifts in addition to the wedding. One of his gifts was a musical automaton hidden in a tortoise-shell case. At the touch of a button, the case opened and a beautiful mechanical bird covered in real feathers appeared and began to sing.

Guests gave practical gifts, too, sized appropriately. Charley received a small billiard table complete with balls, cues, and a rack to match. Lavinia treasured an elegant miniature sewing machine. They also received miniature furniture made of ebony and gold. Drawings of the gifts appeared in newspapers. Many of the gifts were displayed in Manhattan store windows.

TO THE CHURCH

Joyful crowds filled the street in front of Grace Church as one fancy carriage after another pulled up to the church.

Police barred business traffic. Wagons and everyday coaches were forced onto alternate routes. That proved to be a wise decision. As it was, crowds clogged the street and peered out of nearby windows and doorways.

The crowd oohed and aahed as fashionably attired men and women climbed out of their carriages and walked into the church. The men wore formal morning dress: a jacket with tails, a vest, pants, and a top hat. Women in beautifully embroidered and decorated silks of every color imaginable emerged from the carriages. Their dresses swished as they made their way up the steps and into the church. They held their heads high, displaying elaborate bonnets or elegant combs in their ornately styled hair. Jewels sparkled in the morning sun. It was as if each guest was trying to outdo the others.

The organist played as the guests settled into the pews. Every so often, the congregation turned toward the back of the sanctuary to see if the wedding party had arrived. No one wanted to miss the grand entrance of the little celebrities.

The organist played the *William Tell Overture* and several other marches and overtures. At times, the crowd rose expectantly, sure that the little couple was about to enter, but there were several false alarms. At one point, the man entering the church was the Reverend Mr. Willey from Bridgeport, a longtime friend of the groom. He would assist in the ceremony. The crowd took their seats only to rise again when other clergymen arrived. The wedding was about to begin.

Finally, the doors at the back of the sanctuary opened and Barnum himself marched in followed by the Bump and Stratton families. They took seats at the front. The crowd murmured. Surely the little people would arrive soon.

And they did. George Nutt, the best man, led the way. Barnum had talked him into it. George escorted Minnie Warren, the maid of honor. Charles and Lavinia walked hand-in-hand down the aisle behind the best man and the maid of honor.

Everyone struggled to get a good view. Men strained their necks. Ladies stood on tiptoe. Some even dared to climb onto the pews for a better look. Whispered comments and delighted laughter drowned out the strains of the organ:

"Isn't she pretty?"

"How charming."

"How queenly."

"What a manly bearing he has."

"Was there ever anything so lovely?"

"It's like a fairy scene."

The women were entranced by Lavinia's white satin gown. Its train flowed behind her. She wore a wreath of orange blossoms in her hair beneath a snow-white veil. Sunlight sifting through the church windows lighted a diamond star on Lavinia's forehead. Charley gave Lavinia diamonds as his wedding gift. A diamond pin clasped her veil, and there were more diamonds on necklaces, bracelets, and pendants. Charley wore a full-dress suit with a blue vest, white gloves, and highly polished boots. George was dressed in a similar fashion, although his vest was pink. Minnie's white silk dress was decorated with pink rosebuds.

The bride and groom charmed onlookers in their wedding finery.

Lavinia and Charley took their vows before a church full of invited guests.

The wedding party climbed onto a platform especially for the wedding. Order was quickly restored, not only by the presence of two dozen uniformed policemen but also by the ringing voice of the Reverend Willey, who began the ceremony. The congregation settled into their seats as the minister offered a prayer for peace and prosperity for Charles and Lavinia.

The bride's pastor, the Reverend Dr. Putnam, gave Lavinia away in marriage. At that point, according to newspaper reports, the wedding party "knelt in prayer, and the rich sunlight fell through the painted windows upon them."

Charley and Lavinia repeated their wedding vows confidently and in voices loud enough for all to hear, and then, as the minister pronounced them husband and wife, the newlyweds sealed the vows with a kiss.

As the organ played a recessional, the newlyweds progressed down the long aisle and into a waiting carriage. The *New York Times* of February 11, 1863, described the scene outside the church:

> It is not necessary to mention here of the shouts and yells and screeches with which the junior portion of the throng hailed the happy couple as they entered and left the church. Although it may seem ridiculous, yet it is nevertheless true, that hundreds of persons, including adults, ran after the carriage, not diminishing their speed until the Metropolitan Hotel had been reached.

The streets between the church and the hotel were crowded with gawkers. People hung out of windows, crowded onto the sidewalks, and generally did whatever they could to steal a glimpse of the wedding party. And for a moment, at least, the news of war was forgotten in their enthusiasm and joy at being witnesses to at least a bit of the "fairy wedding."

CAKE AND GOOD WISHES

———◇———

At the Metropolitan Hotel, Lavinia changed out of her wedding dress into a dress especially made for the reception. As with the bridal gown, Barnum had spared no expense on her clothing. Madam Ellen Demorest, the leading fashion expert of the time, created most of Lavinia's dresses, including the two for her wedding day. Madam Demorest's Emporium featured beautiful and innovative fashions.

Lavinia's taffeta reception dress shimmered beautifully as the color shifted from pale amber to white and back again. Each panel of the dress featured a different national symbol embroidered into the fabric. There was a rose for England, a laurel for France, a shamrock for Ireland, oak leaves for Germany, grapes for Italy, a thistle for Scotland, and growing corn for America.

Once the bridal party was ready, they were escorted into the grand ballroom and lifted atop the grand piano. At that height, they were face-to-face with their guests.

Charley looked "pleased and joyful, and smiling, and jolly." Both bride and groom were used to being in the spotlight, and they felt comfortable making conversation with their guests. During the two-hour reception, they greeted most of the 2,000 attendees. The wedding cake, a giant fruit basket, and other sweets were displayed. There was plenty to eat.

This newspaper illustration of the reception shows the wedding party greeting guests from atop the grand piano.

Guests wandered from room to room greeting the couple, viewing the gifts, and visiting with one another. An orchestra played in the background as hotel employees did their best to make everyone feel welcome and well cared for. When the guests left, each received a small box containing a piece of the wedding cake. Over 2,000 such boxes had been prepared in advance.

AGE-OLD CAKE

Many guests saved their piece of cake as a souvenir. The Barnum Museum in Bridgeport, Connecticut, acquired one of the boxes, with the cake still inside. A wedding guest had saved it and passed it on to various descendants before someone contributed it to the museum.

A large crowd gathered outside the hotel, hoping that the couple would reappear. They were still there cheering when the New York Excelsior Band arrived to serenade Charley and Lavinia.

At 10:00 PM the band stopped playing. Charles stepped onto a hotel balcony to address the crowd:

Ladies and Gentlemen: I thank you most sincerely for this, and many other tokens of kindness showered upon me today. After being for more than twenty years before the public, I little expected, at this late day, to attract so much attention. Indeed, if I had not become a "family man," I should never have known how high I stood in the public favor, and I assure you I appreciate highly and am truly grateful for this evidence of your esteem and consideration. I am soon off for foreign lands, but I shall take with me the pleasant recollection of your kindness today. But, ladies and gentlemen, a little woman in the adjoining apartment is very anxious to see me, and I must, therefore, make this speech, like myself—short. I kindly thank the excellent band of music for its melody, the sweetness of which is only exceeded by my anticipations of happiness in the new life before me. And now, Ladies and Gentlemen, wishing you all, health and happiness, I bid you all a cordial good-night.

JUST A DISTRACTION?

The next day the wedding was front-page news. The *New York Times*, the *New York Herald*, the *New York Observer*, and other city papers reported on the wedding as a local event. But papers as distant as the *Sacramento Daily Union* in California carried an entire column about the wedding. Weekly magazines like *Leslie's Illustrated News*, *Harper's Weekly*, and even *Scientific American* covered the wedding.

Why? Was it simply a distraction from the war? It was that, but many experts believe that the amount of attention given the "fairy wedding" was far more complicated. Coming as it did in the middle of the Civil War, the wedding was bound up with all the changes in American life. War casualties were mounting. Many men returned home severely maimed; they had lost legs, arms, and the ability to resume their former lives. Others simply disappeared. Their fate was never known.

Over and over in news stories about the wedding, reporters emphasized the physical perfection of the bride and groom. Although they were not of average stature, they were always portrayed as attractive, intelligent, and well mannered. These were characteristics that most 19th-century people admired. The *New York Illustrated News* described Charles as "well proportioned, his head handsomely and naturally developed, and the size of his hands and his feet is in proper proportion to that of his body. He has a fair complexion, light hair, rosy cheeks, and dark eyes." Both Barnum and the press frequently referred to Lavinia as the "little queen of beauty." Did focusing on the beauty of the little people reassure Americans at a time when life seemed uncertain? Perhaps. It's also likely that the wedding created a sense that all was well in a world where such lovely people fall in love and marry. This thought was a comfort in stressful times. The biggest *little* wedding in the world reminded people that love flourishes even in the most trying times and under the most unusual circumstances.

8

AT THE WHITE HOUSE

The day after the wedding, Charley and Lavinia left New York on a wedding tour. They planned to visit Philadelphia; Baltimore; Washington, DC; and their hometowns in Connecticut and Massachusetts.

The couple stopped first in Philadelphia, where they charmed the crowds at the Continental Hotel. From there, they traveled to Washington, DC, and checked into Washington's Willard Hotel, where they planned to hold a reception for guests. They had not expected an invitation to the White House, but that's what awaited them. President and Mrs. Lincoln would expect them the next evening, February 13, for a small gathering.

It's not clear how Mrs. Lincoln came to issue the invitation. Some say that Barnum himself exerted pressure on the Lincolns. Others suggest that Mrs. Lincoln's friends convinced her that it was her duty to entertain

This photograph
of Mary Lincoln
was available as a
carte de visite.

the little people. After
all, they said, if the
queen of England and
other European roy-
alty had welcomed
Tom Thumb into their
palaces, shouldn't the
"wife of the President
of his native country
smile upon him also?" Mary Lincoln began preparing
for a White House reception.

Perhaps Mrs. Lincoln was simply ready to return to
a more active social life. For nearly a year, the White
House had been a somber place. In addition to the trials
of leading a war-torn nation, the Lincolns had suffered
a personal loss. On February 20, 1862, their 11-year-old
son, Willie, had died of typhoid fever, the same disease
that had struck Lavinia during her showboat days. Willie's death devastated the Lincolns.

Gradually, Mrs. Lincoln emerged from mourning.
She said, "My position requires my presence, where my
heart is *so far* from being." So she called on wounded

soldiers in Washington, DC, military hospitals two or three times a week and resumed visiting with friends at the White House on Saturdays. The reception for Lavinia and Charley was quickly organized. Mrs. Lincoln invited five cabinet members, several senators and congressmen, and some Civil War generals. They all brought their families. President Lincoln wore a somber black suit and white gloves on his large hands. Mrs. Lincoln had changed out of mourning clothes into a high-necked pink silk gown with a large hoop skirt decorated with flounces, or ruffles.

A NEWSWOMAN'S REPORT

———•◇•———

Grace Greenwood, who was the first woman to write for the *New York Times*, was present at the reception for Charley and Lavinia. She described the event:

> The reception took place in the East Room; and when, following the loud announcement, "Mr. and Mrs. Charles Stratton," the guests of honor entered from the corridor, and walked slowly up the long salon, to where Mr. and Mrs. Lincoln stood, to welcome them, the scene became interesting, though a little bizarre. The pygmy "General," at that time still rather good-looking, though slightly blasé [unimpressed by his surroundings], wore his elegant wedding suit, and his wife, a plump but symmetrical little woman, with a bright, intelligent

face, her wedding dress—the regulation white satin, with point lace, orange blossoms and pearls—while a train some two yards long swept out behind her. I well remember the "pigeon-like stateliness" with which they advanced almost to the feet of the President, and the profound respect with which they looked up, up, to his kindly face. It was pleasant to see their tall host bend, and bend, to take their little hands in his great palm, holding Madame's with especial chariness [care], as though it were a robin's egg, and he were fearful of breaking it. Yet he did not talk down to them, but made them feel from the first as though he regarded them as real "folks," sensible, and knowing a good deal of the world. He presented them, very courteously and soberly, to Mrs. Lincoln, and in his compliments and congratulations there was not the slightest touch of the exaggeration which a lesser man might have been tempted to make use of, for the quiet amusement of on-lookers; in fact, nothing to reveal to that shrewd little pair his keen sense of the incongruity of the scene.

Lincoln was a well-known storyteller, and often his jokes were at the expense of others. But both Grace Greenwood and Lavinia noted that there was no hint of that in his manners that evening. Lavinia wrote, "Knowing his [Lincoln's] predilection for story telling, I imagined he was about to utter something of a humorous nature, but he only said, with a genial smile, 'Mrs. Stratton, I wish you much happiness in your union.'"

Others congratulated the Strattons, and then "the president took our hands and led us to the sofa, lifted the General up and placed him at his left hand, while Mrs. Lincoln did the same service for me, placing me at her right; we were thus seated between them."

Nine-year-old Tad Lincoln stood beside his mother. He gazed at Lavinia for a few moments, and then he said to his mother, "Isn't it funny that Father is so tall and Mr. and Mrs. Thumb are so little." It was not only that the Strattons were little; Lincoln was particularly tall. He stood six feet, four inches tall and weighed 200 pounds. At the time, the average male height was five feet, eight inches.

It was the president who replied. "My boy, God likes to do funny things. Here you have the long and short of it."

Everyone laughed.

A few minutes later, Tad leaned over and whispered to his mother, "Mother, if you were a little woman like Mrs. Stratton you would look just like her."

Several people nearby overheard. They smiled and agreed. It wasn't the first time, or the last, that the two women would be compared.

In concluding her observations of the reception, Grace Greenwood wrote:

While the bride and groom were taking a quiet prome-
nade by themselves up and down the big drawing room,
I noticed the President gazing after them with a smile
of quaint humor; but in his sorry-shadowed eyes, there

was something more than amusement—a gentle sympathy in the apparent happiness and good-fellowship of this curious wedded pair—come to him out of fairyland.

Tad Lincoln is shown here with his father, President Abraham Lincoln, at about the time Lavinia met him at the White House.

Charley and Lavinia stayed at the White House for about 90 minutes before returning to the Willard Hotel, where they met friends and members of the press. They celebrated well into the night.

VISITING THE TROOPS

The next day, the newlyweds crossed the Potomac River and visited the Union army camp at Arlington Heights, Virginia. Before the war, Arlington had been the 1,100-acre estate of Mary Custis Lee, the wife of General Robert E. Lee. The general had been Abraham Lincoln's first choice to command the Union army, but Lee's loyalties were divided. His home state of Virginia had already seceded from the Union; he was a strong supporter of the Union but loved his state. Lee debated with himself for days. Finally, he declined Lincoln's offer and resigned from the Union army. As he explained to his sister, "With all of my devotion to the Union and the feeling of loyalty and duty of an American citizen, I have not been able to make up my mind to raise my hand against my relatives, my children, my home." On April 22, 1861, Lee accepted command of the Virginia forces of the Confederate army.

Within a month, while General Lee was with his troops far from home, his Virginia estate was surrounded and taken over by the Union army. It became a Union camp. By February 1863, about 150,000 troops

EMANCIPATION PROCLAMATION

Charley and Lavinia's wedding reception was not the first White House social event of the year. On January 1, 1863, the Lincolns held a large New Year's Day reception. On the same day, President Lincoln issued the Emancipation Proclamation. Mary Lincoln was pleased. She believed that the proclamation would be a "rich and precious legacy for my sons."

The Emancipation Proclamation gave freedom to any person held in slavery in the Confederate states. But the proclamation's power was limited: it applied only to the states that had seceded from the Union, and Lincoln had no power to enforce it. The Emancipation Proclamation did not end slavery. It did, however, encourage Union troops by suggesting that their efforts would eventually end slavery. It also allowed black men to join the Union army and navy.

were stationed there. Among them was Lavinia's brother, Benjamin, of the 40th Massachusetts Regiment.

When Lavinia realized how close she and Charley would be to Benjamin's unit, she asked President Lincoln if they could visit the troops. He granted them a pass to enter the camp. When their carriage arrived, soldiers threw their caps into the air, cheered, and shouted greetings. Many had seen General Tom Thumb on one of his cross-country tours. Happy memories lit their faces. Soon these soldiers would be off to battle, and many would not return. Benjamin's commander granted him a few days' leave to accompany the newlyweds north.

Benjamin joined Lavinia and Charley and their staff, which included Charley's agent, his private secretary, and his valet, the male servant who attended to his personal needs. Lavinia's maid traveled with them too. The entourage stopped in Baltimore and New York City before going on to Bridgeport to see the Strattons. From there, they traveled to Middleborough to visit the Bumps. At each stop along the way, they were cheered and toasted in joyful receptions.

MILITARY OVERTONES

In her memoir, Lavinia recounted a conversation that occurred at the White House reception.

"Is General Tom Thumb's name on our Army list?" President Lincoln asked. In other words, had he ever served in the army?

Edwin Stanton, Lincoln's secretary of war, turned to Charley and asked if he'd ever been on active military duty.

Lincoln responded before Charley could. "Oh, his duty now will always be required in the matrimonial field; he will serve with the home guard."

It was a joke, of course. Charley's body size made military service impossible despite the military title in his stage name. During this time in US history, many little people were given grand titles. Some scholars believe that people found comfort in the notion that military commanders were not always big and powerful men leading their sons to war. "General Tom Thumb" and "Commodore Nutt" were comic characters, generating laughter, not fear.

Two weeks after Lavinia and Charley visited Washington, Congress enacted a draft that required all males ages 20–45 to serve in the military. However, there were exceptions. Anyone who could find a substitute or pay the staggering sum of $300 (over $5,000 in today's money) did not have to serve. For many in the North, the Civil War had become a poor man's war, because only the wealthy could afford the fee to avoid military service.

The Confederate government had enacted a draft on April 6, 1862, about a year earlier. All white men ages 18–35 were expected to serve for three years unless their jobs were considered essential. Communities could not afford to lose the services of railroad workers, telegraph operators, teachers, or druggists. In the South, too, wealthy men could hire others to serve until a law passed in December 1863 ended that practice. Thousands of young men left home to fight for the cause—whichever cause they favored—and many never came home again. More than 750,000 Americans lost their lives in the Civil War. Thousands of others suffered disabling injuries.

TRAVELING NEAR AND FAR

The excitement over the "fairy wedding" did not fade overnight. After a short visit with family, Charley and Lavinia returned to New York and took up residence at the St. Nicholas Hotel. The parties continued. Lavinia did not mind the receptions (she was accustomed to standing for long periods and greeting admirers), but the elaborate dinners taxed her patience. It was the custom to wear gloves to dinner and to keep them on while eating. No store-bought gloves fit her, so hers were specially made, which was time-consuming and costly. And eating with gloves on, especially ones that weren't a perfect fit, was difficult.

George and Minnie had been appearing at the American Museum since the wedding. Charley and Lavinia joined them by the end of March. Charley was eager to retire from show business and spend his time at home

This is one of many pieces of sheet music generated by interest in the wedding. Another was called "The Fairy Wedding Waltz."

with his ponies and boats. Lavinia, on the other hand, loved the spotlight. She was eager to get back to work. Eventually, Charley gave in to her wishes.

The four performers spent most of their time at Barnum's American Museum. An advertisement in the *New York Herald* promised that the May 25, 1863, performance would feature all four members of the wedding party in their "wedding costumes" and that some of the wedding gifts would be on display. From time to time they left the museum to appear in Newark, New Jersey, and in Albany and Troy, New York.

Barnum suggested that the four little people take a swing through New England and Canada before going to Europe. He proposed that they employ Sylvester Bleeker, one of Barnum's trusted assistants, as their agent. The little people agreed. They hired Bleeker, whom Lavinia always called Mr. Bleeker, to arrange their travels and appear on stage as master of ceremonies. His wife would serve as wardrobe mistress for the journey. There were lots of dresses and costumes used in the shows.

Mr. Bleeker made the arrangements and the troupe prepared to leave New York. They caught the last train out of the city before violence erupted. Lavinia and Charley were unaware that hundreds of New York City workers planned to protest the draft that Congress had passed the previous month. Only after they left did they read the frightening newspaper reports of the riots. Rioters had paraded through city streets carrying posters and banging metal pans. They had overturned telegraph poles, uprooted train tracks, and attacked black workers and torched their homes. They had even burned the Colored Orphan Asylum on West 44th Street. The children had escaped unharmed, but others who were caught in the riots were not so lucky.

The majority of the rioters were Irish immigrants working in low-paying jobs. If they were drafted, their families risked starvation, and they feared that if and when they returned home, free black workers would have taken their jobs. Innocent black people became their victims. So did wealthy businessmen who could buy their way out of military service. Protestors attacked newspaper offices and prosperous businesses. When the final tally was taken, 119 were dead. Most of them had been rioters. Many of the 300 injured were policemen and soldiers. The riots finally ended when federal troops arrived in New York on July 16, 1863. President Lincoln agreed to lower the number of New York City draftees by half.

Lavinia wrote in her autobiography, "A reign of terror in our own New York seemed incredible. Houses looted, asylums burned, and tracks torn up! Could these things be?" The entertainers were safe but nevertheless uneasy about the horrors that had occurred back home.

ON TOUR

The tour of New England and Canada was a success, in no small part because of the publicity from the wedding.

During their performances, Lavinia sang several solos. Among them was "Annie of the Vale":

> The young stars are glowing,
> Their clear light bestowing,
> Their radiance fills the calm, clear summer night!
> Come forth like a fairy,
> So blithesome and airy,
> And ramble in their soft and mystic light!
> CHORUS: Come, come, come love, come!
>   Come ere the night torches pale!
>   Oh come, in thy beauty,
>   Thou marvel of duty,
>   Dear Annie, dear Annie of the Vale.

She also recited poems, danced, and sang duets with Charley. George and Minnie sang solos too, and the entire company joined in a variety of skits. Both Lavinia and Minnie wore beautiful gowns and exquisite jewelry. They dressed appropriately—as full-grown women, not as little girls—and they carried themselves with dignity and style. Charley and George often appeared in military uniforms befitting their fake military titles.

As Barnum had proposed, Bleeker served as master of ceremonies. He introduced the various acts and stood near the little people as a visual reminder of their diminutive size. The troupe visited with several wealthy and influential Canadians. The money rolled in; so did the invitations to visit other towns and cities.

Lavinia and Minnie dressed elegantly whenever they appeared before the public.

Charley, Lavinia, Minnie, and George took advantage of the opportunity for sightseeing. They toured Montreal, Ottawa, and Toronto. A European trip was on the horizon, but there was still time, Barnum told them, to tour a few more US states.

THE DANGERS OF WAR

The troupe, now called the Tom Thumb Company, continued on to Indiana and Ohio. At the Columbus, Ohio, train station they met General Ulysses S. Grant. He was on his way to Washington to take command of the Union army. His special train car was attached to part of the same train that carried the Tom Thumb Company. Grant sent an aide to ask if General Tom Thumb and his wife would allow him to stop in.

Lavinia and Charley did not hesitate to invite Grant to join them in their compartment. During his visit, he congratulated the newlyweds and reminded Lavinia of their earlier meeting in Galena. He told her that he still had her signed photograph. He had seen Tom Thumb, too, several years before. After a cordial chat, he warned the entertainers not to stray into enemy territory.

Despite Grant's warning, Lavinia was excited by the prospect of being near the fighting. It was not unusual at the time for people to ride out to Civil War battlefields and observe the conflict firsthand. In fact, some brought picnic baskets and ate lunch as the battle raged. Lavinia urged Mr. Bleeker to take the troupe into Kentucky. As it turned out, they did not get near any battlefields, but in Louisville they visited a Union prison for captured rebel soldiers. The troupe of little people took time to speak with the prisoners.

John Wilkes Booth, a respected Shakespearean actor, was also playing in Louisville. His hotel room was directly across from Lavinia's. As they talked, he shared with her his sympathy for the South and the Confederacy. Booth's arguments were not unfamiliar. Lavinia had heard them before among Northerners called Copperheads or Peace Democrats. They wanted peace through a settlement with the South. Most of them lived in Ohio, Indiana, and Illinois. Booth had joined another party in the 1850s: the Know-Nothing party. Their goal was to limit immigration. During the Civil War, Booth served as a Confederate spy. No one knew, of course.

Spies depend on secrecy. As their conversation ended, John Wilkes Booth gave Lavinia a signed photograph.

Lavinia and the company flirted with danger as they traveled through Kentucky and reached the Tennessee border. The Confederate general John Hunt Morgan led his raiders through Kentucky, Ohio, and Indiana that summer. *Harper's Weekly* magazine of August 1862 described Morgan as a "guerrilla and bandit." His aim was to stop Union troops by capturing Union horses, burning bridges, tearing up railroad tracks, and destroying Union supplies. It worked, but the Union cavalry pursued him.

In Middle Tennessee, Bleeker received word that Morgan and his raiders had torn up the railroad tracks just a few miles ahead. Had the problem not been discovered, the train would have derailed, injuring or possibly killing the passengers. Lavinia and the others waited several hours until the tracks were repaired. Lavinia seemed to enjoy such close calls; Charley preferred a quieter, safer existence. Luck traveled with the Tom Thumb Company. They returned safely to New York City after an 11-month tour of Canada and the United States. The trip yielded a profit of $82,000, which is equal to more than $1 million today.

EUROPE AT LAST

Charley and Lavinia had been married for well over a year when they finally set sail for Europe in October

1864. George and Minnie went along, as did the Bleekers and a large staff. The ocean crossing took 14 days, and when they finally reached the dock in Liverpool, England, a crowd of hundreds greeted them.

Fans made it difficult for the little people to leave the hotel each day. Lavinia spent her time doing embroidery. Charley was fascinated. He asked her to teach him to embroider. Together they created several large pieces of embroidery as covers for their dining room chairs. Lavinia explained that these were not the miniature chairs that she and Charley used, but the larger ones they kept to accommodate their friends.

The troupe spent several weeks in London before sailing for France. Only Charley spoke French, so he served as an interpreter. On their return to London, the troupe was summoned to Windsor Castle to entertain the royal family. After they put on their "entertainments," Queen Victoria took Lavinia aside and asked about her family back in Massachusetts. She then said, "I saw your husband many years ago," and shared her memories of Tom Thumb's first visit to the palace.

The Tom Thumb Company was in Europe when they learned of the war's end and the assassination of President Lincoln. Lavinia vividly remembered her meeting with John Wilkes Booth the previous year in Louisville. It didn't seem possible that he had taken such drastic action. She was stunned and deeply saddened. She had Booth's photograph with her. When a British reporter asked her about the assassination, she gave him the photo to use in his story about Lincoln's death. It was the first photo of Booth to appear in a British newspaper.

Many reports coming from the United States unsettled Lavinia. The war had ended but troubles continued, especially in the war-torn South. Men on both sides of the conflict were missing, injured, or dead, and families were trying to rebuild their lives.

New York papers also reported that Barnum's American Museum had burned to the ground. None of the performers or spectators died, but several animals were killed in the fire. Barnum didn't waste time; he reopened the museum in a nearby building.

A HOAX

While they were in England, Lavinia and Charley took part in a hoax of their own. They had been photographed with a baby before leaving New York. Everyone assumed that the child was theirs, and news spread quickly that Mr. and Mrs. Tom Thumb were now parents. As much as they would have loved a child of their own, it never happened. They had "borrowed" a child from an orphanage for a photo.

Lavinia later admitted, "I never had a baby. The exhibition baby came from a foundling hospital [orphanage] in the first place and was renewed as often as we found it necessary. At the age of four our first baby was taller than his father." Eventually, a story circulated that

In this photo, taken in New York before the troupe left for Europe, Lavinia is holding one of the many "borrowed" babies.

their child had "died." That wasn't true either, of course, because there had never been a baby in the first place. It was simply a way to conclude the hoax.

Lavinia spent her free time in Europe sightseeing. She visited the Tower of London and other historical places. The others went along. They enjoyed visiting tourist sights, but wherever they went, they attracted a crowd.

After a year in London, the troupe went on the road. Lavinia wrote in her autobiography that they performed in a total of 208 cities and towns in England, Scotland, Wales, and Ireland. They left Liverpool for America on June 12, 1867.

ⒹANGEROUS ⒿOURNEYS

By July 1867, the four members of the wedding party
were back in New York City performing in Barnum's
new museum, now called the Barnum and Van Amburgh
Museum and Menagerie Company. After a brief series of
performances, Charley and Lavinia returned to Bridgeport. They were wealthy, and Charley didn't hesitate to
indulge in expensive hobbies. He owned several boats
and enjoyed sailing on Long Island Sound. He drove his
buggies and coaches along the country roads. He rode
horseback, too, and bought Lavinia a pony of her own.

Charley owned several properties in Bridgeport,
including the mansion with rooms built to his scale. He
would have been content to spend the rest of his life at
home. After all, he had been a professional entertainer
since the age of four. But Lavinia found travel exciting.
She was far more adventurous than Charley. She loved

her time on stage. "I like the public, and I think the public likes me," she said. If ticket sales were any indication, she was absolutely correct. Wherever the little people performed, ticket sales soared.

Charley, eager to please Lavinia, gave in. He agreed to another tour. Their next trip took the Tom Thumb Company to the South. The Civil War had prevented them from going to many Southern cities. They visited Columbia and Charlestown, South Carolina, as well cities and towns in the south and as far west as San Antonio, Texas.

After the tour, they spent a few months at home. Lavinia enjoyed keeping house and spending time with family, but she missed traveling and the adventures it brought.

Barnum, meanwhile, hatched another plan. On May 10, 1869, he wrote to Sylvester Bleeker.

My Dear Bleeker:

An idea has occurred to me in which I can see a "Golden Gate" opening for the Gen. Tom Thumb Co. What do you think of a "Tour Around the World," including a visit to Australia? The new Pacific Railroad will be finished in a few weeks; you will then be enabled to cross the American Continent to California, thence by steam to Japan, China, British India, etc. I declare, in anticipation, I already envy you the pleasures and opportunities which such a trip will afford.

For the next three days I shall study all maps I can lay my hands upon, and, in imagination, mark you crossing the briny deep to those far-off countries. And as for *gold!* tell the General that in Australia alone (don't fail to go to Australia) he will be sure to make more money than a horse can draw.

It will require great care, judgment, experience, and energy, all of which faculties you possess, to carry such an enterprise to a successful termination.

Talk it over with the "little people." I name you Generalissimo of the invading force in their grand march, and hope you will return with spoils from all the nations of the globe.

Decide quickly! If you consent to undertake the journey, prepare to start next month. Love to all.

Truly yours,
P.T. Barnum

Bleeker read the letter to the little people.

"Never! Never will I go to Australia!" Charley cried.

"Go to Australia?" Lavinia exclaimed. "Our friends would never expect to see us again." Neither George nor Minnie wanted to go either.

At the time, Australia was largely unknown to Americans. Not only was it on the other side of the world, but it was also common knowledge that many Australian settlers had been convicts, shipped to Australia from Great Britain. The last convict ship reached Australia in 1868, only a year before Barnum proposed the trip. In total, 162,000 men and women had been sent to Australia on 806 convict ships. Large parts of Australia were still unexplored, and outlaws called bushrangers attacked travelers, especially those carrying gold.

Mr. Bleeker reminded the troupe that gold had been discovered in Australia in May 1851. Charley's eyes lit up. He reconsidered his initial response. "Vinnie," he said, "it would be very interesting to visit the great Australian gold mines."

Charley may have wavered, but the others did not. Australia was out. Bleeker wrote a contract, which all the members of the Tom Thumb Company signed. They agreed to visit "such cities and towns as the said manager, Sylvester Bleeker, may decide upon" with the exception of Australia.

P. T. Barnum stands behind the Tom Thumb Company, his famous ensemble of little people.

FIRST STOP: THE WILD WEST

On June 21, 1869, the Tom Thumb Company left New York City for their world tour. In addition to the four performers and the Bleekers, they took along a treasurer, an agent, a general assistant, and a doorkeeper to help manage the crowds at the shows. Because they were taking a miniature carriage and a pair of tiny ponies, they also took a groom and a coachman. The coachman was George Nutt's brother, Rodnia, also a dwarf.

Friends and family gathered to wish them well.

"Write often," someone called, tears blurring her vision.

It was exactly as Lavinia had warned. At least some of those gathered feared that the little people would never survive the difficult journey to the other side to the world.

The only reasonable way to travel great distances across America in 1869 was by train. The company averaged 110 miles a day through Pennsylvania, Ohio, Indiana, Missouri, and Nebraska. They stopped at major towns and cities along the way and gave on average two performances each day. They reached Omaha on July 8. So far, the trip had not been that different from previous tours.

On July 11, they stopped for the night at Council Bluffs, Nebraska. Minnie rushed to find Mr. Bleeker. There were American Indians in the hotel courtyard, and they were wearing war paint. She feared imminent attack.

Bleeker followed Minnie to her room where he found all four little people staring out the window in alarm. He turned to Charley and suggested they step outside to visit with the gentlemen.

Charley hesitated. Not Lavinia. She piped up and said, "Why, General, I wouldn't be afraid to go, and I am a woman. If I were a man, I would go in a moment."

What choice did he have? Charley grabbed his hat and followed Mr. Bleeker into the hotel courtyard. The Indians were armed with rifles and scalping knives and dressed in hunting shirts and leggings. They had painted their faces and stuck feathers in their hair.

"Ask them what tribe they belong to," Charley suggested as he clung to Bleeker's coat.

He pointed out that the men seemed not to understand English. He suddenly realized that the Indians assumed Charley was a child. Bleeker stepped aside, removed Charley's hat, and pulled on his beard.

All four Indians broke into huge grins. They walked around Charley and measured him against the height of their rifles. They touched his beard, all in good humor. But when one of the men shifted the position of his knife in his belt, Charley took off running toward the hotel. As Sylvester Bleeker later wrote, he "vanished as if into air." The company later learned that the men were Pawnee warriors in pursuit of a band of Crow Indians.

One stretch of the trip between Nebraska and Wyoming would require a 26-hour train ride through Indian Territory. When the train pulled out the next morning, rumors of Indian attack were as thick as the soot from the train's engine. Several passengers carried weapons. George carried a tiny pistol in his pocket, but Bleeker doubted it would do any damage even if George fired it. Charley suggested that Bleeker buy revolvers for the entire party. He refused and urged calm. None of the company had ever fired a gun before. They would undoubtedly do more damage to themselves than to any would-be attackers.

From the train windows, Lavinia watched herds of graceful antelope. She laughed with delight at the antics of prairie dogs popping out of their dusty burrows to stare at the passing train. With a quick flourish of their tails, they disappeared belowground before she could alert the others.

CHEYENNE AT LAST

Eventually, the Tom Thumb Company reached Cheyenne, Wyoming, a town of 4,000. The troupe performed in an old barn with hastily built board seats. Every seat, no matter how rough, was filled.

The train then carried them into Utah. They performed in many towns, large and small. During each show, Bleeker invited a dozen children between the ages of three and ten to join him on the stage. He had them stand beside Minnie, the smallest of the company. Only the very youngest were her size; all the others stood taller. The audience clapped with delight as their own children stood before them—proof that this was not a hoax.

From Ogden, Utah, the company traveled by stagecoach because the railroad was not yet completed. The stagecoach jolted along rough mountain roads. Lavinia bounced in her seat. There was no good way to hold on, and her feet didn't touch the floor. "Oh, my poor back!" she cried. If only they could stop. But there was no choice except to go on.

Five miles later, she called out again, this time in warning. "I think the linch-pin is lost. I have watched this wheel for the last ten minutes, and it seems to wriggle a great deal."

"Pull up!" Bleeker yelled.

When the driver examined the wheel, he found that Lavinia was right. The linchpin, which holds the wheel onto the axle, was missing. Just a few more turns of the wheel and it would have fallen off. The coach would have toppled over and sent the passengers crashing onto the rocks below. It was the first of many narrow escapes from danger.

The troupe stayed in hotels when possible. They stayed in private homes when the town was too small to support a hotel. None of the lodgings were comparable to the luxuries of New York City hotels or their own homes. They slept on thin straw mattresses with dirty army blankets for covers. They washed with hard yellow soap in tin washbasins and shared one towel with 30 other guests. They shared rooms, and even beds at some stops, because there was no other choice. One hotel, with the elegant name the Cosmopolitan, was built of a few rough boards with canvas curtains strung between sleeping areas.

SPRINGING PANTHER

In Brigham City, Utah, the chief of the local Ute tribe entered the lobby of the hotel where the company was staying. The locals called him Joseph, but his Indian name meant "Springing Panther." Bleeker introduced Springing Panther to the little people. His wife and child waited outside until Lavinia insisted they come in. Springing Panther's wife laughed as she compared her own young child to Minnie. They were about the same size.

That evening, about 40 or 50 members of the tribe rode up and dismounted in front of the hotel. After consulting with Springing Panther, Bleeker asked the little people to stand at the window and greet the group gathered below. Then Bleeker distributed photos of the Tom Thumb Company to the crowd. Rodnia brought the ponies and carriage to the hotel to transport the performers to the concert hall. As soon as the little people were safely inside, the Ute party surrounded the carriage. They formed a unique honor guard. The Indians accompanied the carriage all the way to the concert hall.

Once they arrived, Bleeker invited Springing Panther to attend the show. He eagerly accepted and sent the rest of his tribe back to their camp.

OUTLAWS

The company continued by stagecoach through Utah and into Nevada. In addition to the bumpiness of the ride and the danger posed by steep mountains and deep ravines, outlaw attack was a constant threat. One evening, the company performed at Piper's Opera House in Virginia City, Nevada. Afterward, they retired to their hotel for the evening. Four men stopped by Bleeker's room to warn him of possible danger. Everyone could see that Lavinia and Minnie wore expensive jewelry, they said, and that ticket sales produced lots of cash. *It's dangerous on the road*, the men warned, *and it's important to conceal your valuables when you travel*. Then they asked if the group would be taking the noon stagecoach to Reno. Bleeker nodded.

One of the men said, "When traveling this section, I always conceal my valuables in the lining of the coat; if I can't find an opening, I slyly cut one."

Another asked if Mrs. Thumb carried her own jewels in her trunk. When Bleeker told them that he took care of Lavinia's valuables, the man suggested that he put the watches, money, and diamonds in his hat. The men left, convinced Bleeker had accepted their advice.

Bleeker, however, was wise to their ways. He went to the Wells Fargo office and hired two stagecoaches to convey the company to Reno, not at noon but at 7:00 AM. They reached Reno safely. But the noon stagecoach did not. Four highwaymen attacked it and ordered the male passengers to remove their hats. When they found nothing, they searched the stagecoach, all the while cursing Tom Thumb. Their "good advice" failed to yield the desired reward.

RUNAWAY COACH

After a harrowing trip down steep mountain trails, the company arrived in Sacramento. From there they traveled to San Francisco. They performed at the 2,000-seat Platt's Hall. They gave two or three shows a day for two weeks, every one a sellout.

Before leaving for Japan, the company traveled another 1,000 miles by stagecoach to Oregon, performing in dozens of towns there and in Northern California. Lavinia and Minnie had another close call in Colusa, California, when the driver stepped down from his seat. Lavinia, Minnie, and Mrs. Bleeker remained inside the stagecoach. Something startled the horses and they took off. The driverless coach disappeared in a cloud of dust, while the ladies bounced helplessly inside. Lavinia and Minnie grabbed onto one another. The horses dashed wildly along the road, and Mrs. Bleeker put her arms around the little women to prevent them from being tossed about the coach.

The horses ran about three-quarters of a mile before crashing into a fence at the edge of the road. Mrs. Bleeker jumped out of the coach, holding both Lavinia and Minnie in her arms.

"You saved all our lives, Mrs. Bleeker," Lavinia said. "I did not have any fear of being killed, but I looked every moment for the upsetting, and then that our bodies would be horribly mangled, and I thought what a terrible blow it would be to poor father and mother when they heard of it."

"I am not to be killed so easily," said Minnie. "I thought to myself, 'Go ahead, horses; do your best; I can ride as fast behind you as you can run.'"

Perhaps they remembered the peddler's wagon they had swiped years before.

BEARS

———◇———

Pulling the loaded coaches over the mountains proved difficult work for the horses. Sometimes the little people walked as much as three or four miles along the mountain trails to spare the horses. Lavinia and Minnie often chose to walk along forested ridges just above the road. The pine needles were soft underfoot, and the sheltering trees provided shade. Only later did they learn that grizzly bears and cinnamon bears, a subspecies of the

American black bear, roamed those same woods. Luck had walked with them once again.

After giving shows at many cities in Oregon, the company sailed by steamship from Portland back to San Francisco. After brief visits to San Jose and Stockton, they gave a few more performances in San Francisco. The trip across country, with detours along the way to put on shows, had taken nearly four and a half months. But what an exciting time it had been!

THE OTHER SIDE OF THE WORLD

The ocean voyage to Japan took more than three weeks. The Tom Thumb Company landed at Yokohama on November 30, 1869. Even though none of the company spoke Japanese and few of the Japanese spoke English, the shows were well attended. Everyone enjoyed the novelty of seeing four little people. Whenever Lavinia and Minnie walked through the streets, Japanese women reached out to touch them to see if they were real.

From Japan, the company sailed to China. The miniature carriage and ponies caused a stir in the street whenever the little people traveled to and from the various theaters. Even without an interpreter, the show went on and the audiences were enchanted. In his travel book, Bleeker described one show in Hong-Que:

When Mrs. Stratton sang, the sound of her voice seemed
to entrance them; they sat in breathless attention. . . .
At the conclusion of her song they chatted, they nodded, they laughed and expressed in various ways their
extreme delight. The Commodore in his dancing, drum-
ming . . . and comicalities, excited their risibilities [made
them laugh]; they gazed open-mouthed in wonder at
the General in his characters. The little pantomime play
amused them exceedingly, and their enthusiasm was
unbounded when, after taking a number of little children upon the stage and comparing statures with Minnie, I retained one boy five years old, and placing her
hand in his, she paraded to and fro with him. The little
fellow, with a pigtail touching the floor, strutted about
with her to the immense delight of all. America and
China clasping hands!

The performance was such a success that the company was besieged with offers to perform in other theaters. The company traveled throughout China. From
there they went to Singapore, which was part of the British Empire at the time, and then on to Georgetown, the
capital of Penang, an island in Malaysia.

Lavinia and Minnie were thrilled to go sightseeing.
In Georgetown, they visited a gigantic waterfall and
picked fresh fruits and nuts from tropical trees. This
was the kind of adventure that Lavinia craved, and how
wonderful to share it with Charley and Minnie. They

visited many Asian ports and spent time in Ceylon and India. They toured Buddhist temples and the palaces of kings and rulers. They ate foods that seemed strange and exotic and met people who had never seen any Americans before, let alone such tiny ones.

AUSTRALIA

Although they had not planned to go to Australia, the group relented once they were in Asia. In late January 1870, they set sail for Australia. They traveled by train to the largest cities and towns. However, the only way to reach Southern Australia was by sailing ship or horse-drawn coaches. The journey by sea would take longer, so the company went overland by coach. Bleeker sent the ponies and Charley's carriage by steamship.

Travels in Australia's backcountry proved as difficult as travel in the mountains of the American West. Lavinia and the rest of the troupe often walked for miles to lighten the horses' loads when the roads were deep mud or other conditions proved treacherous. They crossed deserts. They wandered through lush, swampy areas where they saw kangaroos, wallabies, emus, and other creatures they had only imagined before.

At one point, the company had to cross a river swollen by recent storms. They were traveling in a horse-drawn coach, and the water was deeper than the coach driver realized. Water flooded the passenger compartment, reaching clear to the seats. Lavinia and Minnie drew their legs up onto the seat, arms encircling their knees, to stay dry. The horses swam forward, exerting great effort to pull the coach behind them to the other shore.

At one rural stop, the proprietor went to great lengths to offer them an "American supper." The group couldn't help but roar with laughter as he served boiled pumpkin and boiled salt pork. They were hungry enough to eat, but as Lavinia later wrote, "For years after an allusion to an 'American supper' would be greeted with peals of laughter."

They remained in Australia for nine months. They visited 105 different cities and towns and traveled more than 5,300 miles overland. However, Australia was not the end of the journey. The company returned to India and went on to Arabia. They visited Egypt and saw the pyramids. From Egypt, they crossed the Mediterranean Sea to Italy. They visited various European capitals and then landed in England, giving performances in familiar cities and towns.

Lavinia, Charley, George, and Minnie had been on tour for three years and one day. With Mr. Bleeker and their staff, they traveled 55,487 miles by sea, carriage, and train. They gave 1,471 shows in 587 different cities and towns. Not a single accident or illness prevented them from appearing for a scheduled show. It was an exhausting but exhilarating experience. They were happy to return home in June 1871 for a much-deserved rest.

A NEW HOME

———◇———

Charley and Lavinia built a home in Middleborough. Windows reached to the floor, kitchen cabinets were within Lavinia's reach, and the furniture was scaled down. The miniature billiard table they had received as a wedding gift, the small sewing machine, and a miniature grand piano fit perfectly into their new home. They filled several glass cases with beautiful souvenirs of their travels and with their wedding gifts. Charley built a barn next to the house for his racing ponies and small carriages. Lavinia liked fast horses and owned two, which she drove herself. Charley raced up and down the country roads on horseback or in his buggies. He gave Lavinia expensive jewels, which he knew pleased her.

Although Charley always kept meticulous records of their income, he was less careful about spending. He spent lavishly on horses, boats, clothing, and jewelry. The expenses mounted and Lavinia worried, especially when they had to borrow money to buy another boat and to enlarge the stables. Luckily, Mr. and Mrs. Tom Thumb still drew crowds. Touring replenished their bank account.

ANOTHER US TOUR

———◇———

Less than three months after their return from Europe, Charley and Lavinia began touring again, this time in the United States. George and Minnie appeared with them. They visited all 37 states that made up the United States in 1875. During performances, Lavinia often spoke about the troupe's world travels. Few Americans had ever traveled more than a few miles from home. Fewer still

Charley and Lavinia in 1875, when Lavinia was in her mid-30s. Charley had gained weight and grown a few inches taller by this time.

had visited such exotic locations as India or the Pacific Islands. Lavinia's firsthand accounts were exciting.

In 1876, Charley and Lavinia parted ways with P. T. Barnum. Barnum felt that the little people no longer needed him. He was convinced that they had kept him as a partner and given him a share of the profits out of kindness. It seemed unfair. It was a friendly parting, and Lavinia and Charley asked Mr. Bleeker to stay on. He remained their trusted booking agent and manager for as long as they needed him.

MINNIE

Minnie married. She had met Edward Newell, an Englishman who went by the title of Major Newell, in London. Edward was an extremely short man, less than five feet tall, but he was not actually a dwarf. Minnie and Edward traveled with Lavinia and Charley. Edward dazzled audiences with his trick roller-skating.

Other performers joined the troupe as well. Many were little people who sang, danced, and performed in skits. Among them were two Italian brothers, Count Primo Magri and Baron Ernesto Magri. Their stage names were Count Rosebud and Baron Littlefinger.

In 1878, Minnie became pregnant. She was thrilled. Minnie loved children, and she began making doll-sized clothes. She was unaware that her baby might be full-sized or that childbirth posed a special risk for someone her size. She assumed that her baby would be tiny. It wasn't. The baby weighed six pounds at birth. The kind of medical help available today did not exist in 1878. Minnie's tiny body could not handle the stress. She died a few hours after delivering the child. The baby died four hours later. Minnie was 29 years old.

Minnie's death was a terrible blow to the whole family, but especially to Lavinia. The two sisters had a special bond. Lavinia had always felt responsible for Minnie. For the last several years they had been together almost constantly. What would Lavinia do without her little sister? At the funeral, people spoke of Minnie's kindness. Her husband sat by the casket sobbing. Charley stood watch while Lavinia struggled to maintain her composure.

Years later Lavinia said, "It proved one of the greatest trials of my life to go again before the public without her, but it was the lifework marked out for me and I resumed it just as others resume their regular duties after an overwhelming grief."

GEORGE

Years earlier, newspapers had falsely reported that Minnie Warren and George Nutt married. They never did. In the late 1870s, George left the Tom Thumb Company to go out on his own with his brother, Rodnia. They went to San Francisco, where the brothers performed with a comic opera company.

George never married. Some claimed that after losing Lavinia to Charley, he vowed to live life as a bachelor. He started several businesses without much success. In 1881, he organized a troupe called Tally Ho. He planned to put on his own light operas, but a few months later he became ill and returned to New York. He died within a few weeks, at age 37.

"I Belong to the Public"

Alone now, Lavinia and Charley toured the country with Bleeker as manager. By that time, Barnum was in the circus business. In 1881, he offered Lavinia and Charley a year's contract with the "Greatest Show on Earth." They gave it try. But parading around a circus ring and living in makeshift quarters didn't appeal to either Lavinia or Charley. They left after their contract was up and returned to touring with Bleeker and his wife.

In January 1883, they were performing in Milwaukee, Wisconsin. Bleeker had booked rooms at the Newhall House. Late that night a fire started on the first floor of the hotel. It spread up the elevator shaft to the upper floors. The entire building was engulfed in flames.

Lavinia and Charley were sleeping when someone pounded on their door. Charley leaped out of bed and

In this 1881 photo, Lavinia and Charley pose on a theatrical
balcony. She was 40 years old at the time.

opened the door to a frantic policeman, Officer O'Brien. Smoke filled the room. Lavinia, now fully awake, rushed to the window. The hotel was burning! Flames lit the predawn sky. Was there any escape?

Their room was on the third floor directly above the hotel's main entrance. Officer O'Brien pried open the window. Firemen extended a ladder and signaled Charley to climb down first. O'Brien followed, carrying Lavinia.

They were safe, but many others were not. By the time most guests realized that the building was burning, there was no way out. Several of the maids had climbed onto the roof. They screamed for help. Guests, trapped in their rooms, jumped out windows onto the stone pavement below. For many, it was a deadly choice.

Charley and Lavinia stood among the falling ashes, watching as flames consumed the hotel. They listened to the screams of the doomed and watched firefighters struggle to control the inferno. What had happened to the Bleekers? Their room was one floor above Lavinia and Charley's.

They learned later that Mr. Bleeker had tied strips of the bed sheets together to lower his wife to the balcony. But she lost her grip and fell. She was cut and bruised. She broke an arm and leg and dislocated a hip. Rescuers carried her into Lavinia and Charley's room and from there, lowered her with ropes to the ground. Mr. Bleeker slid down the sheet rope to the balcony. From there, he climbed down the fire ladder to safety. He was uninjured, but Mrs. Bleeker died of her injuries 10 days later. Seventy-nine of the hotel's 300 registered guests died in the fire. Many others suffered serious injuries.

Charley and Lavinia were devastated. They had narrowly escaped with their own lives. They had lost the valuables in their room, including about $1,000 in cash. But the worst shock came from witnessing the tragedy and losing Mrs. Bleeker, who had become a dear friend. The night's horrors hit Charley especially hard. Lavinia later wrote, "The General never recovered from the shock of that terrible ordeal."

CHARLEY

Lavinia and Charley limped home to regain their strength, but Charley remained unwell. After a few months, Lavinia resumed the tour while Charley stayed in Middleborough. On July 15, 1883, he suffered a stroke. Lavinia rushed back to Charley, but she arrived too late to bid him a final farewell.

General Tom Thumb's death at age 45 made news around the world. Thousands mourned his passing. Charley had grown portly in later years. He'd even grown several inches taller. But in the public's mind, he was still the tiny tyke who toured the world with P. T. Barnum. Nearly 10,000 people came to pay their respects at his funeral. Most waited outside the church because there was no room inside. Lavinia sat in the front row surrounded by her family. P. T. Barnum cut short a visit to Canada in order to attend.

Lavinia was only 42; she had assumed she and Charley would have many more years together. She was devastated by his death and could not imagine spending

Lavinia, wearing mourning clothes, was devastated by Charley's death.

the years ahead without him. Looking back on their life together, she wrote, "I never knew a person so entirely devoid of malice, jealousy or envy; he had the natural instincts of a gentleman. He was kind, affectionate and generous. He had great sympathy for children and was ever ready to do anything to make them happy. . . . Our married life was a happy one."

Now, Charley was gone and so was Minnie. Lavinia was alone in a world that had always seemed too big. She moved her tiny furniture across the street to her brother's house. She received several offers of employment from amusement companies across America, but she informed everyone that she intended to retire and live a quiet life in Middleborough.

SECOND CHANCES

——◇——

Three months later, while visiting friends in Bridgeport, Lavinia asked Barnum for advice. She felt she could trust his wisdom. After all, both she and Charley had always considered him a close friend and advisor.

Don't quit, he cautioned. His own early retirement brought great unhappiness. Barnum had returned to work and felt Lavinia should do the same. He turned to Sylvester Bleeker and said, "Take her out! Take her out!" He meant that Lavinia should go back on tour; performing before the public would help her recover from Charley's death.

Lavinia accepted his advice and returned to work. She did not go alone. Mr. Bleeker remained by her side. So did her little dog, Topsy, who traveled with her for 13 years. He eventually became part of the show. Lavinia described Topsy in these words: "faithful as a companion, reliable as a guard, curled in my trunk tray, quiet and observant in cars and stations." In a 1906 newspaper interview, reporter Helen Dare noticed that Lavinia had a pair of doves in a cage and a monkey in her hotel room. Lavinia had always loved animals, and she took her pets along on tour.

Lavinia surrounded herself with other little people. Several, like Count Primo Magri and his brother Baron Ernesto, had traveled with the Tom Thumb Company prior to Charley's death. Soon after Charley died, the count sent Lavinia a letter of condolence, which she appreciated.

In the following months, Lavinia often met the brothers at various shows. She came to think of the count as a brother. But over time, their relationship deepened. He proposed; she accepted.

Her second wedding was smaller than her first; it did not make headlines. The newlyweds traveled to the count's native Italy and spent the summer there with his family.

By the end of the summer, Lavinia was eager to return home and settle down in Middleborough. Primo Magri was a real count, so Lavinia gained the title of countess. Even so, she continued to refer to herself in advertisements for her shows as "Mrs. Tom Thumb." The name helped to draw crowds. She began writing her autobiography in the early 1900s and used both names in the title.

The Autobiography of Mrs. Tom Thumb
by Countess M. Lavinia Magri
formerly Mrs. General Tom Thumb.

LIFE AS A COUNTESS

For several years, Lavinia, Primo, and Ernesto toured the United States, giving performances with various companies. Mr. Bleeker remained at her side. The crowds were not as large as those who had come to see the Tom Thumb Company. Many of those in the audience had seen Lavinia when they were children. Now they brought their own children or grandchildren to meet someone they admired.

Lavinia and Primo made several trips to Europe. As she grew older, travel became more difficult. Although she had planned to retire after 50 years in show business, it proved impossible. Money was tight, and Primo was not wealthy. It was true that Lavinia and Charley had earned lots of money over the years, but they had spent freely and saved little. In later years, Lavinia had to sell many of her precious wedding gifts. She even sold her expensive jewels, replacing them with cheap imitations.

This 1890 photo shows Lavinia with Primo and his brother Ernesto (right) in show clothes.

Lavinia and the Magri brothers continued to tour for several years. In the early 1900s, Primo and Lavinia spent several summers at the Dreamland amusement park on New York's Coney Island. They joined other little people in an exhibit called Lilliputia. Nearly 300 little people lived in the specially constructed community. Most of them had been recruited from other circuses or "freak" shows. The popular name of the Coney Island attraction was "Midget City." The term *midget* had always angered Lavinia. She resented being called a midget. It was insulting. She always referred to herself as simply a "little woman." However, a job was a job, and Lavinia and Primo needed the money.

HOME AT LAST

When she finally retired to Middleborough, Lavinia became an active member of many organizations, including the Daughters of the American Revolution. She was proud of her roots, especially of her ancestors who had participated in the Revolutionary War.

She was "Aunt Vinnie" to many children in Middleborough and enjoyed time with her family, friends, and pets. She and Primo appeared in shows throughout the region, often to aid local causes.

In 1915, Lavinia and Primo went to Hollywood. They appeared in a 35-minute silent movie called *The Lilliputians' Courtship*. Lavinia played the role of Lady Petite. The count was Uncle Tiny Mite. By this time, Lavinia was 74 years old. She had become plump. Although she still dressed well and took great care of her appearance, she was no longer the "little queen of beauty" the public had flocked to see in 1863.

The same year that the film came out, 1915, Lavinia and the count opened a small general store in

Middleborough. Many of the customers who said they came to buy ice cream really came to see Lavinia. She posed for pictures and signed autographs. This was her public, and she wanted to please them.

Lavinia celebrated her 78th birthday with 150 friends. Less than a month later, she fell ill. She died in Middleborough on November 25, 1919. Her death was reported in several papers around the country. She was buried next to Charley in a Bridgeport, Connecticut, cemetery.

When Lavinia agreed to leave teaching and enter show business, she had been seeking adventure. She found it when she met Barnum, married Charles Stratton, and performed on the world's stages. As Lavinia wrote, "I belong to the public. . . . Appearing before audiences has been my life. I've hardly known any other."

Lavinia Warren may have been a little woman, but she lived life on a grand scale.

ACKNOWLEDGMENTS

This is a true story, at least to the extent that I could determine the truth from historical reports. Much of the story comes directly from Lavinia herself, whose autobiography provides many details about her adventurous life. Although she seldom discussed her political or social convictions, there is no doubt about her love for Charley and her admiration for P. T. Barnum and Sylvester Bleeker. She relied on Bleeker's account of the Tom Thumb Company's travels, as did I. Barnum's autobiographies, if not altogether reliable, contain fascinating accounts of Charley and Lavinia's courtship and wedding. So do newspaper accounts written at the time.

History comes alive through historical documents and artifacts. I want to extend special thanks to Middleborough (Massachusetts) Historical Association president Doug Vantran and board members Dot Thayer,

Gladys Beals, Cynthia McNair, and Nancy Gerdraitis. These dedicated volunteers spend untold hours preserving the history of Lavinia and her Middleborough neighbors. The association maintains the Middleborough Historical Museum, a treasure trove of Lavinia lore. My visit there was a highlight of my research.

So, too, was my visit to the Barnum Museum in Bridgeport, Connecticut, where curator Adrienne Saint-Pierre guided me through the Tom Thumb collection, which includes a piece of Lavinia's wedding cake still in its original box. Libby Fox, reference/adult services librarian at the Middleborough Public Library, and Elizabeth Van Tuyl, of the Bridgeport History Center, a department of the Bridgeport Public Library, were generous with their time and expertise.

The amazing photographs in this book come from the collections of the Library of Congress, the Bridgeport Public Library, the special libraries of Syracuse University and the University of Pittsburgh, the Public Library of Cincinnati and Hamilton County, and the Anacostia Community Museum. I appreciate the work that librarians and archivists do to maintain and share these fascinating photos and drawings.

I am grateful to the excellent team at Chicago Review Press. Editor Lisa Reardon shared my vision in bringing Lavinia's story to life for today's young readers. Thanks also to Sarah Olson, who designed the jacket (yes, readers do choose a book by its cover), and to project editor Ellen Hornor and copyeditor Sharon Sofinski, who polished the manuscript. Errors that remain are mine alone.

My Fargo, North Dakota, critique group (Linda Sand, June Dordal, Tory Christie, Kristy Olsgaard, and Terrie Enslow) guided my revisions with their insightful comments. Also invaluable were the comments of my first reader, Adeline Raum, who offered a young person's perspective and insights. Thanks as always to my husband, Richard, for his continued patience, encouragement, and love. You've made my life an adventure!

TOM THUMB WEDDINGS

Beginning in the late 1800s, children began reenacting Charley and Lavinia's wedding in ceremonies called Tom Thumb weddings. Children as young as two and as old as 10 dressed in wedding clothes to participate in mock wedding ceremonies. Sometimes they used a script, learned speaking parts, and rehearsed the wedding as a play. Churches, schools, and social clubs sponsored the Tom Thumb weddings.

Throughout the early and mid-20th century, Tom Thumb weddings were popular in both the North and the South. They continue today, although not as frequently as in the past. Children from many different religious and ethnic groups have participated.

Sometimes a child acts the role of minister; sometimes the church's pastor performs the ceremony. Some groups rent small tuxedoes and purchase special dresses for the event. The bride and groom exchange rings made of candy, plastic, or cheap metal. The bride may wear a plastic tiara and fake jewels.

In 1898, Walter H. Baker & Company of Boston, Massachusetts, published a script called "The Tom Thumb Wedding." It is still available. In the introduction, the author states:

This photo from the 1940s shows children at a Washington, DC, church participating in a Tom Thumb wedding.

This entertainment may be given by any number of children from three to seven years of age. . . . Forty or fifty should be secured at least, if at all possible. . . . The tiniest little folks may with wonderful ease be trained to take the various parts.

In addition to the script itself, the pamphlet includes directions for costumes and instructions on how to stage the procession and the wedding ceremony.

However, many groups make up their own script. For example, in some, the minister pronounces the bride and groom "friends for life." In others, vows include promises "to share your milk, to share your cookies, and an occasional Bubble Yum." In one 1983 ceremony, the minister told the congregation:

Dearly beloved. We are gathered here to join these wee little people in make–believe matrimony, here in the sight of all their friends, parents and relatives, to share in some fun. Anyone crazy enough to be upset at such a good time, let him speak now, and be embarrassed by the stares from the whole congregation.

Sometimes the "weddings" are designed as fundraisers. For example, a 2007 event at Shiloh Baptist Church in Decatur, Illinois, raised funds for a youth trip. Other times the mock weddings are purely for entertainment purposes and include a picnic or potluck supper. Some groups use the weddings to teach children proper etiquette. After a 1991 Tom Thumb wedding at Cadman Congregational Memorial Church in Brooklyn, New York, one woman said, "It gives the children something to do; it keeps them off the streets."

Children who participate seem to have mixed reactions. One young groom said, "I am happy it is over with." Another commented, "This was practice for me, so I can see how it will really go later on." Generally, the girls seem to enjoy the ceremonies more than the boys, and parents and grandparents enjoy them most of all.

These children participated in a Tom Thumb wedding in the early 1900s.

QUESTIONS TO PONDER

1. Why do you think that Lavinia agreed so readily to become a "curiosity?" Do you think you would have made the same decision? Why or why not?

2. What unique problems did Lavinia and Charley face as people of short stature? How did they overcome those difficulties?

3. Because Charley became an entertainer at a very young age, he felt that he missed out on childhood. What did he lose in the process? What is the value of play? Are childhood friendships important? Why?

4. What are the advantages and disadvantages of allowing children to perform in public? Imagine that you are the parent of a young child who is offered a job in show business. Would you allow it? Why or why not?

5. Barnum made a fortune deceiving the public. Do you consider him an admirable character? Why or why not?

6. Today, people often want government protection from schemes and scams designed to cheat them out of their money. Should the government protect individuals from "humbugs" or does responsibility rest with each individual to make wise choices? Should some schemes be against the law? Try to think of examples.

7. Charley and Lavinia gained fame and fortune because of their unique physical characteristics. How are they like or unlike many of today's celebrities who use their bodies for the same purpose? For example, compare today's high-fashion models to Lavinia. Are there similarities?

8. Consider the effects of entertainment on a nation at war. Do certain kinds of entertainment appeal more to us during wartime than during times of peace? If so, what are they and why do we prefer them? Should entertainment be an escape from reality or a spur to deeper thinking? Think of examples to support your opinions.

TIME LINE

January 4, 1838	Charles Stratton is born in Bridgeport, Connecticut.
October 31, 1841	Mercy Lavinia Warren Bump is born in Middleborough, Massachusetts.
Fall 1841	P. T. Barnum opens the American Museum in New York City.
June 2, 1849	Huldah Pierce Warren Bump, called "Minnie," is born in Middleborough, Massachusetts.
1857–1858	Lavinia teaches school in Middleborough.
1858–1861	Lavinia is a "living curiosity" on the Floating Palace.

February 1861	Lavinia returns to Middleborough to spend time with her family.
July 1862	Barnum goes to Middleborough to meet Lavinia.
Fall 1862	Lavinia moves to New York City.
December 1862	Lavinia goes to Boston and first meets Charles Stratton.
January 1863	Lavinia begins holding levees at the American Museum.
	Charles Stratton courts Lavinia and proposes marriage.
February 10, 1863	Lavinia Warren marries Charles Stratton.
February 13, 1863	Lavinia and Charley attend a reception at the White House.
March 1863	After a brief visit home, Lavinia and Charley return to work at the American Museum.
July 1863	Lavinia and Charley leave on a tour of Canada and New England.
October 29, 1864	The Tom Thumb Company leaves for Europe.
June 1865	Barnum's American Museum is destroyed by fire; Barnum rebuilds.

June 12, 1867	The Tom Thumb Company leaves England for the United States.
November 1867	The Tom Thumb Company tours Southern states.
June 21, 1869	The Tom Thumb Company leaves for California.
November 4, 1869	The Tom Thumb Company leaves the United States for Japan.
November 30, 1869	The Tom Thumb Company arrives in Yokohama, Japan.
June 22, 1871	The Tom Thumb Company returns from the world tour.
July 23, 1878	Minnie Warren dies in childbirth at age 29.
1881	Lavinia and Charley travel with the Barnum & Bailey Circus.
January 10, 1883	Newhall House burns to the ground; Lavinia and Charley escape; Mrs. Bleeker is severely injured.
July 15, 1883	Charles Stratton dies at age 45.
1884	Lavinia returns to work, appearing with the Magri brothers.
April 6, 1885	Lavinia marries Count Primo Magri.

1915	Lavinia and Primo star in *The Lilliputians' Courtship*; they open a general store in Middleborough.
November 25, 1919	Lavinia dies at age 78.
October 31, 1920	Count Primo Magri dies at age 71.

NOTES

CHAPTER 1: LIVING LIFE SMALL

"To the memory of my": Countess M. Lavinia Magri, *The Autobiography of Mrs. Tom Thumb (Some of My Life Experiences)* (Hamden, CT: Archon Books, 1979), dedication.

"What shall I do with you?": Magri, *Autobiography*, 37.

"Get up! Go 'long" through *"We were in high glee"*: Magri, 38.

"The youngest even was far above me in stature": Magri, 38.

CHAPTER 2: A CURIOUS OPPORTUNITY

"My heart failed me": Magri, 41.

"I was with her": Magri, 41.

"one of the most extraordinary": *New York Commercial Advertiser*, December 23, 1862, quoted in Magri, 51.

"I thought I could sing": Helen Dare, "Mrs. Tom Thumb as I Saw Her," *San Francisco Call*, February 18, 1906.

"In those years there was": Magri, *Autobiography*, 42.

"Early as it was, we were awakened": Magri, 43.

"Our terror soon increased": Magri, 43.

CHAPTER 3: DRIFTING TOWARD WAR

"*I instinctively drew back*": Magri, 44.
"*a most chivalrous and kindly gentleman*": Magri, 176.
"*Whether my size did more*": Magri, 46.
"*we can do better*": Magri, 47.

CHAPTER 4: MOVING ONTO THE WORLD STAGE

"*Is it real or is it humbug?*": Neil Harris, *Humbug: The Art of P.T. Barnum* (Chicago: University of Chicago Press, 1981), 77.
"*There was no picture so beautiful*": P. T. Barnum, *Struggles and Triumphs; or, Forty Years of Recollections of P.T. Barnum, Written by Himself* (Hartford, CT: J. B. Burr, 1870), 346.
"*abundant and wholesome attractions*": P. T. Barnum, *The Life of P. T. Barnum Written by Himself* (Urbana: University of Illinois Press, 2000) (originally printed by Redfield, 1855), 63.
"*Now and then some one*": Barnum, *Struggles*, 142.
"*I little thought when we accepted*": Magri, *Autobiography*, 49.
"*Yesterday we saw a very pretty*": *New York Tribune*, quoted in Magri, 50–51.
"*I disclaim all vanity*": Magri, 50.
"*P. T. Barnum, Esq. Dear Sir*": Magri, 52.
"*the rise and fall in history*": "John Albion Andrew," *Gale Biography in Context, Dictionary of American Biography* (New York: Charles Scribner's Sons, 1936).
"*I had heard of General Tom Thumb*": Magri, *Autobiography*, 49.

CHAPTER 5: CHARLEY

"*He was the smallest child*": Barnum, *Life of P. T. Barnum*, 220.
"*Good evening, Ladies and Gentlemen!*": Barnum, *Struggles*, 177.
"*After dinner we saw the greatest curiosity*": A. H. Saxon, *P. T. Barnum: The Legend and the Man* (New York: Columbia University Press, 1989), 132.
"*You know, I never had much*": Alice Curtis Desmond, *Barnum Presents General Tom Thumb* (New York: Macmillan, 1954), 210.

CHAPTER 6: FRIENDS OR LOVERS?

"I remember myself": Magri, *Autobiography*, 53.

"It is well that war is so terrible": Robert E. Lee, quoted in Roy Blount Jr., "Making Sense of Robert E. Lee," *Smithsonian* 34, no. 4, July 2003, 58.

"Her size is that of a child": Sketch of the Life, Personal Appearance, Character and Manners of Charles S. Stratton, the Man in Miniature, Known as General Tom Thumb, and His Wife, Lavinia Warren Stratton, Including the History of Their Courtship and Marriage, with Some Account of Remarkable Dwarfs, Giants, & Other Human Phenomena, of Ancient and Modern Times. Also, Songs Given at Their Public Levees (New York: Samuel Booth, 1874), 8.

"Mr. Barnum, that is": Barnum, *Struggles*, 586.

"Miss Warren, who dislikes affectation": *Sketch of the Life*, 12.

"I received an invitation from President Lincoln": Barnum, *Struggles*, 572.

"To whom?": Barnum, 587.

"It was very pleasant": Barnum, 591.

"I wish I were going over": Barnum, 594.

"We are engaged!": Barnum, 597.

"Do it yourself, General" through *"I hope you may"*: Barnum, 599.

CHAPTER 7: THE BIGGEST LITTLE WEDDING

"a quartette of the most wonderful": Magri, *Autobiography*, 67.

"I could afford to give them": Barnum, *Struggles*, 601.

"Not for fifty thousand dollars": Barnum, 602.

"As the General and myself": Magri, *Autobiography*, 58.

"Everybody in the church": Magri, 58.

"One thing is certain": Letter reprinted in *Middleborough (MA) Gazette*, February 7, 1863.

"Isn't she pretty?": *Sketch of the Life*, 17.

"knelt in prayer, and the rich sunlight": *New York Times*, February 11, 1863.

"It is not necessary": "Loving Lilliputians; Warren-Thumbiana. Marriage of General Tom Thumb and the Queen of Beauty. Who They Are, What They Have Done, Where They Came from, Where They Are Going. Their Courtship and Wedding Ceremonies, Presents, Crowds of People. The Reception the Serenade," *New York Times*, February 11, 1863.

"pleased and joyful": "Loving Lilliputians."

Many guests saved their piece: The Barnum Museum preserved the piece of wedding cake. View the photo and learn more at http://collections.ctdigitalarchive.org/islandora/object /60002%3A1414.

"Ladies and Gentlemen": *Sketch of the Life*, 22.

"well proportioned, his head handsomely": *New York Illustrated News*, February 21, 1863, 242.

"little queen of beauty": *Sketch of the Life*, 11.

CHAPTER 8: AT THE WHITE HOUSE

"wife of the President of his native country": Elizabeth Keckley, *Behind the Scenes or Thirty Years a Slave, and Four Years in the White House* (New York: Oxford University Press, 1988), 128.

"My position requires my presence": Ruth Painter Randall, *Lincoln's Sons* (Boston: Little Brown, 1955), 180.

"The reception took place in the East Room": Grace Greenwood, "Reminiscences of Abraham Lincoln: Lincoln's Reception to Tom Thumb—His Favorite Books—In His Coffin," in *Abraham Lincoln: Tributes from His Associates—Reminiscences of Soldiers, Statesmen, and Citizens* (New York: Thomas Y. Crowell & Sons, 1895), 111.

"Knowing his [Lincoln's] predilection": Magri, *Autobiography*, 61.

"the president took our hands": Magri, 61.

"Isn't it funny that Father": Magri, 62.

"While the bride and groom": Greenwood, "Reminiscences," 112.

"with all of my devotion to the Union": Robert E. Lee, quoted in "Timeline: The Life of Robert E. Lee," *American Experience*, PBS,www.pbs.org/wgbh/americanexperience/features/time line/lee-timeline.

"rich and precious legacy for my sons": Randall, *Lincoln's Sons*, 181.

"Is General Tom Thumb's": Magri, *Autobiography*, 62.

CHAPTER 9: TRAVELING NEAR AND FAR

"A reign of terror in our own New York": Magri, 65–66.

"The young stars are glowing": *Sketch of the Life*, 32.

"I saw your husband many years ago": Magri, *Autobiography*, 79.

"I never had a baby": Dare, "Mrs. Tom Thumb."

CHAPTER 10: DANGEROUS JOURNEYS

"I like the public": Dare, "Mrs. Tom Thumb."

"My Dear Bleeker": Sylvester Bleeker, *Gen. Tom Thumb's Three Years' Tour Around the World, Accompanied by His Wife—Lavinia Stratton, Commodore Nutt, Miss Minnie Warren, and Party* (New York: S. Booth, 1872), 9.

"Never! Never will I go to Australia!": Bleeker, *Gen. Tom*, 9.

"Vinne . . . it would be very interesting": Bleeker, 10

"such cities and towns": Bleeker, 10.

"Write often": Bleeker, 11.

"Why, General, I wouldn't": Bleeker, 12.

"vanished as if into air": Bleeker, 13.

"Oh, my poor back!" through *"Pull up!"*: Bleeker, 24.

"When traveling this section": Bleeker, 35.

"You saved all our lives": Bleeker, 41.

CHAPTER 11: THE OTHER SIDE OF THE WORLD

"When Mrs. Stratton sang": Bleeker, 70.

"for years after an allusion": Magri, *Autobiography*, 143.

"It proved one of the greatest trials": Magri, 169.

CHAPTER 12: "I BELONG TO THE PUBLIC"

"The General never recovered": Magri, 169.

"I never knew a person": Magri, 169.

"Take her out! Take her out!": Magri, 170.

"faithful as a companion": Dare, "Mrs. Tom Thumb."

"The Autobiography of Mrs. Tom Thumb": Magri, *Autobiography*, title page.

"I belong to the public": Dare, "Mrs. Tom Thumb."

TOM THUMB WEDDINGS

"This entertainment may be given": Lucy Jenkins, *The Tom Thumb Wedding and The Brownies' Flirtation: Two Unusual Entertainments for Children* (Boston: W. H. Baker, 1898), 3.

"friends for life": Fawn Vrazo, "Wee Do—Youngsters Are Joined in Mock Matrimony," *Philadelphia Inquirer*, July 1983.

"Dearly beloved": Vrazo, "Wee Do."

"It gives the children": "Tom Thumb Weddings: Only for the Very Young," *New York Times*, June 16, 1991.

"I am happy": "Tom Thumb Weddings."

"This was practice for me": Sheila Smith, "Friends for Life: Children Get a Preview of Wedding Day at Shiloh Baptist Church," *McClatchy-Tribune Business News*, June 11, 2007.

BIBLIOGRAPHY

BOOKS

Barnum, P. T. *The Life of P. T. Barnum Written by Himself.* New York: Redfield, 1855.

Barnum, P. T. *Struggles and Triumphs; or, Forty Years of Recollections of P.T. Barnum, Written by Himself.* Hartford, CT: J. B. Burr, 1870.

Bleeker, Sylvester. *Gen. Tom Thumb's Three Years' Tour Around the World, Accompanied by His Wife—Lavinia Stratton, Commodore Nutt, Miss Minnie Warren, and Party.* New York: S. Booth, 1872.

Blyer, Julius, and Herman Blyer. *Burning of the Newhall House.* Milwaukee, WI: Cramer, Aikens and Cramer, 1883.

Bogdan, Robert. *Freak Show.* Chicago: University of Chicago Press, 1990.

Chemers, Michael M. *Staging Stigma: A Critical Examination of the American Freak Show.* New York: Macmillan, 2008.

Cross, Helen Reeder. *The Real Tom Thumb.* New York: Four Winds, 1980.

Desmond, Alice Curtis. *Barnum Presents General Tom Thumb.* New York: Macmillan, 1954.

Fitzsimons, Raymund. *Barnum in London.* New York: St. Martin's, 1970.

Fretz, Eric. "P. T. Barnum's Theatrical Selfhood and the Nineteenth-Century Culture of Exhibition." In *Freakery: Cultural Spectacles of the Extraordinary,* edited by Rosemarie Garland Thomson. New York: New York University Press, 1996.

Greenwood, Grace. "Reminiscences of Abraham Lincoln: Lincoln's Reception to Tom Thumb—His Favorite Books—In His Coffin." In *Abraham Lincoln: Tributes from His Associates— Reminiscences of Soldiers, Statesmen, and Citizens.* New York: Thomas Y. Crowell & Sons, 1895.

Keckley, Elizabeth. *Behind the Scenes or Thirty Years a Slave, and Four Years in the White House.* New York: Oxford University Press, 1988.

Kunhardt, Philip B. Jr., Phillip B. Kunhardt III, and Peter W. Kunhardt. *P. T. Barnum: America's Greatest Showman.* New York: Alfred A. Knopf, 1995.

Magri, Countess M. Lavinia (Mrs. Tom Thumb). *The Autobiography of Mrs. Tom Thumb (Some of My Life Experiences).* Hamden, CT: Archon Books, 1979.

Romaine, Mertie E. *General Tom Thumb and His Lady.* Taunton, MA: William S. Sullwold, 1976.

Saxon, A. H. *P. T. Barnum: The Legend and the Man.* New York: Columbia University Press, 1989.

Sketch of the Life, Personal Appearance, Character and Manners of Charles S. Stratton, the Man in Miniature, Known as General Tom Thumb, and His Wife, Lavinia Warren Stratton, Including the History of Their Courtship and Marriage, with Some Account of Remarkable Dwarfs, Giants, & Other Human Phenomena, of Ancient and Modern Times. Also, Songs Given at Their Public Levees. New York: Samuel Booth, 1874.

ARTICLES

Dare, Helen. "Mrs. Tom Thumb as I Saw Her." *San Francisco Call*, February 18, 1906.

Day, Danielle. "His Aunt Was Mrs. Tom Thumb." *Middleborough Antiquarian* 31, no. 1 (Summer 1993): 4–5.

Franino, Jean. "'The Biggest Little Marriage on Record': Union and Disunion in Tom Thumb's America." *American Quarterly* 67, no. 1 (March 2015): 189–217.

Lincoln Lore (Bulletin of the National Life Foundation). "Tom Thumb Visits the White House." No. 1467 (May 1960): 1–3.

New York Times. "Loving Lilliputians; Warren-Thumbiana. Marriage of General Tom Thumb and the Queen of Beauty. Who They Are, What They Have Done, Where They Came from, Where They Are Going. Their Courtship and Wedding Ceremonies, Presents, Crowds of People. The Reception the Serenade." February 11, 1863.

Smith, Sheila. "Friends for Life: Children Get a Preview of Wedding Day at Shiloh Baptist Church." *McClatchy-Tribune Business News*, June 11, 2007.

IMAGE CREDITS

Page 9: Library of Congress, LC-DIG-cwpbh-02976

Page 11: Bridgeport Public Library

Page 16: The Collection of the Public Library of Cincinnati and Hamilton County

Page 18: Darlington Digital Library, Special Collections, University Library System, University of Pittsburgh

Page 23: Library of Congress, LC-USZ62-127588

Page 30: Library of Congress, 7LC-DIG-pga-00785

Page 35: Middleborough Historical Association, Middleborough, Massachusetts

Page 38: Library of Congress, LC-DIG-ppmsca-35586

Page 40: Library of Congress, LC-DIG-ppmsca-09854

Page 50: Bridgeport Public Library

Page 56: From *The Life of P.T. Barnum* (1855)

Page 64: Ronald G. Becker Collection of Charles Eisenmann Photographs, Special Collections Research Center, Syracuse University Libraries

Page 66: Ronald G. Becker Collection of Charles Eisenmann Photographs, Special Collections Research Center, Syracuse University Libraries

Page 72: Author's collection

Page 80: Library of Congress, LC-USZ62-48351

Page 81: Bridgeport Public Library

Page 84: Ronald G. Becker Collection of Charles Eisenmann Photographs, Special Collections Research Center, Syracuse University Libraries

Page 89: Library of Congress, LC-DIG-ppmsca-19221

Page 93: Library of Congress, LC-USZ62-8117

Page 99: Library of Congress, LC-USZ62-100754

Page 103: Ronald G. Becker Collection of Charles Eisenmann Photographs, Special Collections Research Center, Syracuse University Libraries

Page 108: Bridgeport Public Library

Page 112: Ronald G. Becker Collection of Charles Eisenmann Photographs, Special Collections Research Center, Syracuse University Libraries

Page 127: Ronald G. Becker Collection of Charles Eisenmann Photographs, Special Collections Research Center, Syracuse University Libraries

Page 132: Ronald G. Becker Collection of Charles Eisenmann Photographs, Special Collections Research Center, Syracuse University Libraries

Page 135: Bridgeport Public Library

Page 139: Ronald G. Becker Collection of Charles Eisenmann Photographs, Special Collections Research Center, Syracuse University Libraries

Page 146: Frederick Douglass Dwellings Collection, Anacostia Community Museum Archives, Smithsonian Institution, donated by members of Southeast Voices

Page 148: Library of Congress, LC-DIG-hec-30334

INDEX